DIGITAL SAT STUDY GUIDE

Land Your Dream Scholarship with this Practical Exam Prep for a Perfect 1560+ Score! Includes Mock Exams & Hundreds of Practice Questions for Math, English, Science & More

Herbert Presley

DISCLAIMER

The questions and content presented in this book have been meticulously developed by the author using a variety of reputable educational resources, including Digital SAT practice materials. These materials have been adapted, modified, and created to align with the educational objectives of this study guide.

It is crucial to understand that while the utmost care has been taken to ensure the quality and accuracy of the questions and content, they are not endorsed by the College Board, the organization responsible for the Digital SAT examination. Furthermore, the questions and content in this study guide may not be representative of actual Digital SAT exam questions, and no assurances are made regarding their similarity to questions that may appear on the official Digital SAT exam.

Moreover, any resemblance between the questions and content in this study guide and those found on official Digital SAT exams is entirely coincidental. The primary purpose of this study guide is to provide students with comprehensive practice and instruction to support their preparation for the Digital SAT exam.

By utilizing this study guide, readers acknowledge and understand that the questions and content are for educational purposes only and are not intended to replicate the exact content of the Digital SAT exam. The author and publisher assume no responsibility for any consequences arising from the use or misuse of the materials presented herein.

TABLE OF CONTENTS

APPENDIX: ADDITIONAL RESOURCES 1

PART I: WARM UP 3

Digital SAT Introduction 3

Introduction 4

    Benefits of the Digital SAT 5

    What to Expect on Test Day 5

    Test Day Logistics 5

    Cracking The Digital Sat: Basic Principles 6

PART II: READY 11

Master the Reading & Writing Section 11

Introduction 12

Reading Questions & Type 14

Advanced Skills 19

    Vocabulary: Playing the Greatest Hits 20

    Down to two (or More): Mastering POE 23

    Poetry: Keeping you cool 26

    Sentence Function: Understanding Why Sentences Are Included 28

Comprehensive Reading Drill 38

Rules Question 42

PART III: STEADY 47

Master the Math Section 47

Introduction 48

Fundamentals 50

Algebra Fundamentals & Strategies 56

    Variables, Expressions & Equations 57

    Basic Equation Solving 58

Functions & Graphing 62
    Systems of Equations 63
    Nonroutine Problem Types 67
    Controlling Test Anxiety 68
    Digital Adaptability 69
    Effective Problem-Solving Strategies 70

Functions and Graphs 73
    Applications of Functions and Graphs 75

Arithmetic 78
    Numbers and Operations 78
    Properties of Arithmetic Operations 80
    Applications of Arithmetic in Daily Life 82

Geometry and Trigonometry 85
    Geometry 86
    Trigonometry 89
    Applications of Geometry and Trigonometry 90

PART IV: GO 93

Take the Digital SAT 93

Practice Test 94

Conclusion 149

APPENDIX: ADDITIONAL RESOURCES

To further enhance your understanding and application of the concepts discussed in this book, we have compiled a comprehensive appendix that includes additional materials, detailed examples, and extended case studies. These resources are designed to provide you with practical tools and deeper insights into the strategies and practices that are essential for mastering the Digital SAT.

We encourage you to utilize these materials to expand your knowledge base and apply what you've learned during the real Exam.

How to get the download:

To download the appendix, please Email us directly at:

info@taronegroup.com

With this Code: **DIGISAT**

You'll receive the link to a secure download page where you can access the materials.

The appendix is formatted in a user-friendly manner, allowing you to easily navigate through the additional content and integrate this information with the main topics covered in the book.

Thank You for Your Interest!

We appreciate your interest in expanding your knowledge and skills through the supplementary materials provided. The appendix is designed to be a valuable tool in your educational journey, offering additional content that aligns with the strategies discussed throughout this book. Whether you are a student preparing for the Digital SAT, a teacher helping students succeed, or simply someone interested in mastering standardized tests, these resources are tailored to support your growth and proficiency.

PART I
WARM UP
Digital SAT Introduction

INTRODUCTION

Congratulations on taking the first step toward your college journey! This guide will serve as a comprehensive introduction to the Digital SAT, equipping you with the knowledge and strategies to excel on this crucial exam.

The Digital SAT, introduced in 2023, is a revamped version of the traditional paper-and-pencil SAT. It assesses your critical thinking, reading comprehension, writing, and mathematical problem-solving skills in a digital format. This online test aims to provide a more streamlined and efficient testing experience while retaining the core functionalities of the original SAT.

Here's a breakdown of some key changes:

- **Delivery:** The exam is administered entirely online on a computer provided by the testing center.
- **Interface:** The test uses a user-friendly interface with features like passage highlighting, answer marking for later review, and an on-screen calculator for the math section.
- **Timing:** The Digital SAT has a total testing time of approximately 2 hours and 14 minutes, significantly shorter than the previous 3-hour paper-based version.
- **Scoring:** The scoring scale of 200-800 for each section (Reading, Writing and Language, and Math) remains unchanged.

Benefits of the Digital SAT

The Digital SAT offers several advantages over the traditional format:

- **Accessibility:** The digital format caters to students who are more comfortable with technology and online testing environments.
- **Efficiency:** Online scoring streamlines the process, potentially leading to faster results.
- **Flexibility:** The test interface allows for easier navigation and review of passages and answers.
- **Environmental impact:** It reduces reliance on paper-based materials, promoting an eco-friendlier approach.

What to Expect on Test Day

The College Board offers official practice tests online that closely replicate the look and feel of the actual exam. Utilize these resources to get accustomed to the interface and navigation tools. Take diagnostic practice tests to gauge your proficiency in each section. Focus on areas that require more improvement. Practice time management skills so you can allocate appropriate time for each section and question. Learn effective strategies for approaching different question types, like passage-based reading and problem-solving in math.

Test Day Logistics

Plan to reach the testing center well before your scheduled appointment to undergo check-in procedures and familiarize yourself with the testing environment. Bring a valid photo ID, a valid school ID (optional), and any approved testing accommodations you may have been granted. Remember, personal items like phones or watches are strictly prohibited.

The testing center will provide noise-canceling headphones and a computer to take the exam.

Breakdown of the Digital SAT

The Digital SAT is divided into three sections: Reading, Writing and Language, and Math. Each section is timed separately, and there are short breaks in between.

- **Reading and Writing (64 minutes (two 32-minute modules)):** This section assesses your ability to analyze and comprehend a variety of reading passages from different genres like literary nonfiction, science, and history, written communication skills and your understanding of English grammar and usage. You will encounter multiple-choice questions that test your understanding of the main ideas, supporting details, author's purpose, vocabulary, and reasoning employed in the passages. It also consists of multiple-choice questions focused on identifying errors in grammar, sentence structure, and style, as well as a writing prompt that requires you to craft an essay on a specific topic.

- **Math (70 minutes (two 35-minute modules)):** This section is divided into two parts. Both sections assess your problem-solving abilities in areas like algebra, geometry, statistics, and data analysis. The questions range from multiple-choice to grid-in formats, where you enter your numerical answer directly into the provided grid.

Cracking The Digital Sat: Basic Principles

Having familiarized yourself with the Digital SAT format and structure, let's delve into the essential principles you can utilize to conquer this crucial exam. These principles form the bedrock of a successful test-taking strategy, applicable across all sections – Reading, Writing and Language, and Math.

Mastering Time Management

The Digital SAT is a race against the clock. Each section has a predetermined time limit, and effective time management is paramount to maximizing your score. Here's how to master this art:

- *Pre-planning:* Allocate time for each section based on its length and your perceived strengths and weaknesses.
- *Pacing:* Maintain a steady pace throughout each section. Don't get bogged down on any single question and learn to skip and come back later if needed.
- *Time Awareness:* Regularly glance at the on-screen timer to ensure you're on track. Don't get caught spending too much time on a single passage or question.
- *Strategic Leaving:* If you're completely stuck on a question, educated guessing is better than leaving it blank. Utilize any remaining time strategically to make educated guesses on unanswered questions.

Active Reading and Annotation

The Reading section hinges on your ability to engage with the passages and extract key information actively. Here's how to excel in this domain:

- **Pre-reading Skim:** Before diving into the details, skim the passage quickly to grasp the central theme and the author's purpose.
- **Active Annotation:** Utilize the highlighting function to mark key points, vocabulary words, and transitions. This will aid in revisiting crucial information and making connections.
- **Question-Focused Reading:** Don't just passively read the passage. Approach it with the specific questions in mind, anticipating the type of information you need to extract.
- **Review and Revisit:** Utilize the breaks between sections to revisit your highlighted sections and confirm your understanding of the passages.

Strategic Approach to Writing

The Writing and Language section assesses both your writing skills and your understanding of grammar. Here's how to tackle this section effectively:

- **Grammar Fundamentals:** Brush up on your grammar skills, focusing on areas prone to errors like subject-verb agreement, pronoun usage, and comma placement.
- **Question-Type Familiarity:** Familiarize yourself with the different question types in this section, such as identifying sentence errors improving sentence structure, and word choice.
- **Time Management for Writing Prompt:** Allocate sufficient time for planning and writing your essay. It's crucial to brainstorm, organize your thoughts, and write a clear and concise response.
- **Proofreading:** Before submitting your essay, utilize the remaining time to proofread for any typos, grammatical errors, or inconsistencies.

Math Strategies for Success

The Math section tests your problem-solving skills in various mathematical areas. Here are some key strategies to crack the code:

- *Conceptual Understanding:* Focus on building a strong foundation in mathematical concepts. Rote memorization won't suffice; genuine understanding is key to tackling diverse problems.

- **Strategic Use of Calculator:** Utilize the on-screen calculator effectively for complex calculations, but don't become overly reliant on it. Practice mental math for simpler problems to save time.
- **Test the Answers (Plugging In):** For multiple-choice questions, after solving a problem, try plugging in the answer choices to see which one yields the correct result.
- **Estimation:** Develop estimation skills to assess the reasonableness of your answer choices quickly. This can be particularly helpful when time is of the essence.

Practice Makes Perfect

The key to success on the Digital SAT lies in consistent and focused practice. Here's how to make the most of your preparation time:

- **Quality Practice Tests:** Take official College Board practice tests and timed section-specific practice tests to simulate the actual exam experience.
- **Analyze Your Performance:** After completing practice tests, analyze your performance in each section to identify your strengths and weaknesses.
- **Focus on Weaknesses:** Dedicate more time and effort to areas that require improvement. Seek additional practice problems or resources to address specific weaknesses.
- **Review Strategies:** Continually refine your test-taking strategies based on your practice experiences. What worked well? What could be improved?

Develop Test Routines

Following consistent routines or processes when tackling different question types is important for accuracy and efficiency. Here are examples:

For multiple-choice questions:

1. Read questions and all answer choices carefully
2. Eliminate clearly wrong answers
3. Compare remaining choices methodically
4. Select answer confidently

For grid-in math questions:

1. Read questions and set up work clearly on paper/notes
2. Solve following proper order of operations
3. Enter the numeric answer neatly in the box provided
4. Check work before submitting

For reading comprehension passages:

1. Read the passage actively and take brief notes
2. Read questions fully before revisiting the passage
3. Refer directly to the cited text when answering
4. Select one clear answer, not multiple possibilities

Following proven routines anchors preparation habits to your digital test performance. Mastering these foundational techniques will help you make the most of opportunities and crack the Digital SAT. Preparation, focus, and confidence will lead to success.

PART II
READY
Master the Reading & Writing Section

INTRODUCTION

While assessments provide useful data, the overarching goal of education should be developing lifelong competencies. Part II of this guide focuses on cultivating higher-order thinking skills through hands-on, interactive learning experiences rather than surface-level test preparation.

Key domains will include competencies identified by employers as most important for career success in the 21st-century workplace, such as critical thinking, complex problem-solving, collaboration, and self-management. Through project-based challenges, students will strengthen these abilities while exploring topics that engage their interests and goals.

Rather than isolated skill-building, competencies will be developed through authentic, transdisciplinary projects. Students will work in teams to research issues, evaluate sources, design innovative solutions, and present findings. Along the way, they will self-reflect on strengths, set personal learning targets, and provide peer feedback to support continued growth.

Instructors will scaffold this process through guidance, feedback, and connection to underlying cognitive science principles. Regular formative assessment will emphasize competency demonstration and progress, replacing reliance on standardized exams. Students will curate portfolios showcasing competencies attained and explore future applications.

The use of emerging technologies like virtual/augmented reality, digital storytelling, coding, and multimedia tools will enhance engagement and allow innovative demonstration of higher-order thinking. Community partnerships may involve applying learning to help address real issues.

This innovative instructional model holds the potential to maximize learning through student-driven exploration of personally meaningful topics. Deeper cognitive skills take shape through iterative, experience-based processes rather than surface-level memorization. Students gain ownership of their ongoing development as independent scholars and problem-solvers.

Rather than test preparation alone, the overarching goal is empowering all individuals to take ownership of and actively direct their own educational journeys. By cultivating self-directed, inquiry-driven learning from an early age, students gain the higher-order thinking skills and self-awareness necessary to continually adapt their knowledge and skills throughout lifelong career and social changes. This model fosters competencies shown to transfer most effectively to dynamic post-secondary, workplace, civic and personal landscapes.

Core abilities like critical thinking, complex problem-solving, collaboration, and self-management allow graduates to learn quickly on the job, develop innovative solutions, and engage as dynamic citizens. They can readily acquire new technical knowledge and skills as fields continuously evolve. Researchers have demonstrated these "meta-competencies" correlate most closely with career satisfaction and success in our highly interconnected, globally complex modern world.

By shifting focus from isolated testing toward demonstration of competencies through hands-on, iterative projects, this approach also bolsters students' acquisition of growth mindsets. Learners gain self-confidence as they come to see abilities like reasoning and creativity as skills that can continuously strengthen through effort over time. This resilience and motivation to continuously stretch oneself serve individuals well throughout life's unpredictable, changing challenges and opportunities.

If implemented conscientiously across varied learning environments, with ample support for both students and educators alike, this model promises profoundly beneficial and far-reaching impacts. Not only could it help maximize learning outcomes and close socioeconomic opportunity gaps, but by cultivating lifelong, self-directed learners prepared to shape disruption, it could strengthen communities and democracy for generations to come. Its effects would reverberate broadly to enhance our shared global future.

Let us now explore in more depth how this approach can support all students in continually strengthening critical abilities for lifelong success. Upcoming chapters will outline core processes, suggest project examples, and address facilitating competency-driven learning at various grade levels.

READING QUESTIONS & TYPE

Reading is a fundamental skill that is learned at a young age and continues to be developed throughout life. The ability to read allows one to gain knowledge from written text and to learn about new ideas, stories, concepts, and information. While reading itself is a basic skill, understanding and comprehending what is being read can take many forms. This paper will explore questions related to reading comprehension as well as different types of reading questions. It will delve into the purpose of various reading questions and how they assess different levels of understanding. Overall, this comprehensive overview aims to provide an in-depth look at reading questions and the way they are categorized.

Types of Reading Questions

There are several main types or categories of reading questions that are commonly used to evaluate reading comprehension. These include literal, inferential, evaluative, and applied questions. Each of these questions their own purpose in assessing what was read and will be defined in further detail below.

Literal Questions

Literal questions, also sometimes called factual or right there questions, focus on explicit details, facts, or information that is clearly stated in the text. The answer to a literal question can be found verbatim or almost verbatim in the passage. These types of questions test basic recall and require the reader to look back at the text to find answers. Examples of literal questions include questions about the setting, characters, specific events, numbers, definitions, or other concrete details from the reading. Literal questions are usually lower-order questions that assess the most basic level of comprehension.

Inferential Questions

While literal questions aim to measure remembering or recalling details, inferential questions evaluate a reader's ability to go beyond the literal meaning of the words and make logical deductions based on clues from the text. Inferential questions require the reader to piece together various details and facts in order to arrive at a conclusion that is implied but not explicitly stated. These types of questions ask the reader to make inferences, draw conclusions, identify cause-and-effect relationships, or understand motivations based on evidence in the passage. Answering inferential questions demonstrates a deeper level of comprehension by showing the reader can connect ideas and read between the lines.

Evaluative Questions

Evaluative questions take comprehension a step further by assessing a reader's ability to make a judgment about the quality, credibility, accuracy, or significance of ideas or content in the text. These types of questions prompt the reader to analyze, critique, or determine the worth or importance of information based on evidence and reasoning. Evaluative questions often begin with words like "justify," "determine," "support," "analyze," "criticize," "rate the importance of," or "provide evidence for or against." At a higher cognitive level than simple recall or inference, answering evaluative questions demonstrates a depth of critical thinking about what was read.

Applied Questions

The most advanced type of reading questions are application questions. These questions challenge readers to take what they have learned from the text and apply it to a new, hypothetical, or real-world situation that requires higher-order thinking. Applied questions prompt the reader to use information, principles, or ideas from the reading and demonstrate how to implement, carry out, or apply them in a practical sense. These types of questions may ask how the content could be used, how new examples compare to what was described, or how the details could inform real decisions or problem-solving. Answering applied questions shows a comprehensive understanding and the ability to transfer understanding to novel contexts.

Using Headings to Organize Questions

When developing reading questions for assessment purposes, it is important to incorporate a variety of question types in order to thoroughly evaluate comprehension skills. A common practice is to organize questions using descriptive headings that indicate the level and type of thinking required to answer each question. This helps readers understand what is being assessed and guides them on how deeply they need to engage with the text. Some common heading options include:

Recall & Detail

These headings signal the questions are targeting basic recall of facts, details, examples, definitions or events directly stated in the passage.

Main Ideas & Themes

Headings like these prompt the reader that questions will relate to broad central topics, concepts or underlying messages conveyed in the text.

Inference & Interpretation

Inference questions expect the reader to go beyond the lines and make conclusions supported by evidence, so headings advise thinking in more analytical terms.

Critical Evaluation

Headings informing the inclusion of evaluative questions help prepare readers for judgment calls about content qualities or claims being made.

Application & Integration

Application headings forewarn questions may necessitate connecting ideas to new relevant scenarios or problem-solving contexts.

Proper headings guide readers on what level of comprehension is required to answer groups or clusters of questions rather than guessing at each individual item. This promotes a more strategic reading approach.

Developing Questions at Multiple Levels

When constructing different types of reading questions, it is important to sample questions from low to high levels of thinking to fully encompass the breadth of comprehension assessment. A best practice approach incorporates a mix of question types at varied cognitive demand levels.

For example

A reading passage and accompanying set of questions could include:

- 2-3 literal or factual recall questions
- 2 inferential questions requiring evidence-based conclusions
- 1 evaluative question assessing quality or claims
- 1 higher-order applied question

Balancing easily with more difficult questions in this manner helps ensure all readers can show some understanding while still being challenged. It also comprehensively evaluates the full spectrum of comprehension, from simple details to evaluative and applied thinking. Over-relying on only lower-level recall questions fails to adequately measure critical analysis, application, and higher reasoning expected of proficient readers. A good selection of question types represents the broad scope of what readers should understand and be able to do with what they read.

Additionally, grouping lower and higher questions together, rather than all lower followed by all higher questions, maintains engagement throughout the assessment. Readers must sustain attention and deeper thinking rather than being allowed to disengage after easier initial questions. A thoughtfully constructed mix reinforces monitoring one's comprehension on an ongoing basis as intended.

Short Answer vs. Multiple Choice

A final consideration regarding reading questions involves their structure or format. There are two main types used – short answer questions and multiple choice. Both have advantages and disadvantages depending on the comprehension skills and levels being assessed.

Short answer questions, as the name implies, require the reader to generate an original response of a sentence or two directly answering the question. This format is better for evaluating abilities like summarizing, paraphrasing, making connections, and applying ideas since it does not provide answer options as hints. However, the short answer also leaves more room for ambiguity or variance in grading responses. Multiple choice questions, where test takers select the correct response from a few options, are more consistent and objective to score. However, multiple choice can be answered correctly through test-wise guessing skills rather than actual understanding at times. Used together, short answer and multiple choice cover more ground in comprehension evaluation and mitigate any flaws inherent to just one format alone. A combination of both provides optimal assessment.

ADVANCED SKILLS

Advanced reading skills enable comprehension of sophisticated written works at the most profound levels through the implementation of strategies that extend far beyond surface-level decoding of individual terms. Gaining true mastery over intricate texts necessitates honing a refined array of cognitive mechanisms for extracting complete, nuanced significance. This comprehensive examination aims to illuminate specific capacities central to achieving the highest echelons of reading competency. Discrete sections will thoroughly investigate essential techniques like vocabulary expertise, adept paragraph analysis, and other methods for gleaning full comprehension from even the most challenging pieces of literature, scientific reports, or other written mediums. With diligent and consistent refinement of these sophisticated abilities through targeted practice, concentration, and application to an assortment of materials, one is capable of evolving into an unparalleled reader fully equipped for academic success and professional accomplishment, as well as enriched personal enrichment and satisfaction gained through independent learning pursuits. It is the goal of this writing to illuminate the process through a detailed review of advanced reading strategies, models for implementation, and inspiring examples of their impacts.

Vocabulary: Playing the Greatest Hits

Vocabulary is the foundation upon which comprehension is built. A strong working knowledge of terms empowers communication, problem-solving, memory, and learning across disciplines. However, vocabulary expansion requires sustained, active effort beyond initial exposure to make words stick long-term. This paper explores a vital yet commonly overlooked advanced skill – regularly reinforcing lexical knowledge through meaningful repetition akin to musicians playing their greatest hits. Sections detail techniques for incorporating favorite vocabulary authentically into daily life to fortify retention and enrich understanding over the lifespan. With dedication to this strategic approach, individuals can develop formidable vocabularies elevating capabilities.

The Case for Repetition

While introducing new terms represents progress, fleeting encounters alone prove insufficient for ownership. Research indicates vocabulary thrives when newly learned words undergo repetitive rehearsal in context. Sporadic studying forgets information quickly, but revisiting words aids their transition from short-term to long-term memory. This reinforces connections in the brain and fosters word recognition in more applications. Periodic reactivation maintains knowledge that would otherwise decay without maintenance over months. Committing favorite vocabulary to "heavy rotation" through thoughtful integration strengthens command.

Flashcard Finesse

Flashcards offer an accessible starting point, though solely quizzing definitions risks redundancy. Advanced practice repurposes flashcards for active engagement. Design colorful, portable decks categorizing terms by subject. Quiz definitions occasionally, but primarily focus on incorporating words creatively into examples and mini-stories. Imaginative scenarios spark lasting associations compared to rote memorization. Write sentences demonstrating various parts of speech or word forms. Pairing words with visual imagery makes them more memorable. Sharing unique flashcard creations with others multiplies reinforcement through social interaction.

Strategic Conversation

Casual conversation provides an authentic venue for recycling prized words. Extend discussions by thoughtfully sprinkling in recently reviewed terms. Define words succinctly when others inquire, further cementing your own understanding. Modify typical responses using a thesaurus to substitute advanced synonyms. Text, email, and chat similarly present low-pressure environments for sprinkling vocabulary. Just avoid stilted overuse. Subtle, natural integration improves communication while recycling words frequently in low-stakes ways. Transitioning words learned into everyday dialogues strengthens command.

Internal Monologues

Replaying info subvocally benefits retention, too. Audio recordings allow immersing in vocabulary anywhere via headphones. Yet silent rehearsal through visualization and self-talk also proves worthwhile. Recall terms' definitions while commuting, chores, or exercise. Imagine using words conversationally or creatively applying them to internal monologues about plans and interests. Pondering "what if" scenarios primes the mind through association. Regular brain rehearsals reinforce words' meaning and usage, strengthening neural pathways without outward effort.

Writing Reinforcement

Purposeful writing lifts vocabulary integration beyond casual mentions by requiring deeper processing. Tailor stylistic exercises like poetry, dialogue, descriptions, or short stories around favorite terms. Draft emails, posts, and articles, including strategic words. Editing reinforces precision as alternative phrasing emerges. Maintain notebooks compiling words thematically. Journal entries provide low-pressure outlets for exploring personal reflections and goals framed through advanced terminology. Whether shared publicly or privately, various styles of writing strengthen word banks through creative expression.

Recreational Reading

No vocabulary tutorial compares to recreational texts. Literature, magazines, and online materials immerse readers in context-rich language modeled by experts. Underlining prized words and their surrounding sentences aids retention. Copying elegant phrasing into commonplace books spreads inspiration. Discussing plots using advanced terms further scaffolds understanding. Whether fiction, biography, or news, stimulating reading feeds the mind. Revisiting old favorites refreshes knowledge without pressure. Pleasure texts motivate review while cultivating advanced literacy through entertainment. Their sophisticated yet authentic vocabulary provides endless reinforcing material.

The Benefits of Perpetual Playlists

Frequent recall through varied channels keeps words dancing on the lips and sharp in cognition. Regular reinforcement transfers terms efficiently from short-term to durable long-term memory stores. Recursive intake gradually personalizes definitions through subjective associations. Confidence emerges in communicating precisely and articulately using personal vocabulary hit lists. As reference libraries expand over time, command of advanced terminology empowers critical thinking, nuanced self-expression, and informed contributions across life pursuits. Playing the greatest hits develops an advanced skillset to last lifelong. With creativity and consistency, personalized word playlists fortify the capacity for continued learning, problem-solving, and engagement with complex ideas.

Advancing with Authentic Practice

Maintaining relevance motivates long-term commitment to this model. Refresh vocabulary libraries periodically based on evolving interests and environmental changes to retain enthusiasm. When discovering a field merits deeper investigation, update lexicons accordingly. Utilizing new terms improves communication within burgeoning areas of focus. Periodic self-tests gauge retention to identify words requiring additional practice. However, repetition requires long-term discipline, and small doses fitted within natural routines compound powerfully. With authentic integration matched to developmental stages, personalized flashcards transform into formidable vocabularies empowering advanced skills.

Down to two (or More): Mastering POE

Grappling with advanced texts often involves comprehending intricate vocabulary with limited contextual clues. In such ambiguous situations, the strategy of Process of Elimination (POE) proves invaluable for deducing unknown term meanings. This paper explores the methodical POE approach and its vital role in comprehending sophisticated language. Sections detail guidelines for systematically analyzing response options to rule out implausible choices and narrow viable answers down to two or more possibilities. With dedicated practice applying POE logic, advanced readers can gain understanding even from passages that historically left them perplexed.

Defining Process of Elimination

POE refers to the logical and systematic cognitive process of considering each potential answer choice presented for an unknown or ambiguous vocabulary term within a given reading passage or assessment question. The reader must then carefully analyze and leverage all available evidence, contextual hints, and reasoning provided—whether explicitly stated or implicitly inferred—in order to methodically evaluate and eliminate response options that seem implausible, factually inaccurate, or unlikely based on a close comparison against subtle nuances within both the choices themselves as well as the surrounding content clues.

Rather than aimless guessing or random selection when direct definitions remain obscure, POE utilizes an organized framework to facilitate a step-by-step deduction of probable meanings through a process of elimination. It relies on the advanced critical thinking skills of scrutinizing each response under a microscope while also gaining deeper comprehension from re-examining implications within the broader context. POE empowers discerning the most credible potential solution(s) by process of elimination after logically ruling out alternatives deemed less tenable based on rigorous analysis and inference from even minimal supporting details.

Establishing the POE Mindset

Adopting the optimal POE frame of mind also necessitates patience. With contexts often sparse and nuances easy to miss initially, rushing to firm conclusions will likely result in premature eliminations, missing crucial subtle hints. Taking time to fully immerse in subtle details within responses, passage language, and structural frameworks allows inferences to evolve organically rather than forcing hasty judgments. Revisiting eliminated options with an open yet questioning perspective enables previously overlooked nuances to emerge on second consideration. Like carefully peeling back layers of an onion, the POE process demands an unhurried approach, allowing each round of evaluation to build upon the last. Only by establishing an attitude tolerant of uncertainty, embracing layers yet unworried by time constraints, can POE's thoughtful logical analysis unfold smoothly to arrive at the most well-supported determinations, even when absolutes remain elusive. A rushed or impatient mindset risks missing opportunities inherent to POE's thoughtful resolution of sophisticated ambiguities.

A Systematic POE Process

The deductive POE process follows a logical step-by-step methodology. Thoroughly completing each stage before moving to the next helps ensure a rigorous analysis.

Step 1) Carefully read all contextual clues provided in full, whether explicit definitions, references, or implicit hints about setting themes or technical language patterns. Similarly, read each response option fully to gain a thorough baseline understanding of nuances within both the context and potential meanings, without this full conceptual foundation, preliminary elimination risks being premature.

Step 2) Note any answer choices containing obvious factual errors, logical fallacies, or inconsistencies when directly contradictory evidence exists within the context. These responses can immediately be ruled out due to clear implausibility. However, avoid dismissals without a clearly explicated rationale.

Step 3) Closely reconsider response definitions and context clues, delving into plausible connotations, technical nuances like prefixes/suffixes, shades of implied meaning, and how potential cognates may connect semantic roots to hints. This probing scrutiny helps expose the feasibility of remaining denotations.

Step 4) Revisit context, rereading with each viable option substituted, evaluating logical sentence/paragraph flow or consistency with broader allusions and framework. Inconsistencies reveal defective options for rule-out.

Step 5) If, after rigorous analysis, exactly two potential answers remain as equally convincing options based on all available evidence and context clues, acknowledge that both responses currently warrant consideration and merit further investigation due to limitations within the provided context. Do not hastily settle on a singular choice or default answer when the rationale remains inconclusive.

Step 6) If, upon rigorous and methodical evaluation, no response options can reasonably be eliminated from consideration based on the identification and explanation of flaws within the rationale connecting the choices to the provided contextual hints, it becomes necessary to re-examine the passage details with an open mind. Look for possibly overlooked nuances, technical implications, subtle references, or meaningful linguistic features that could break the current analytic stalemate if insightfully reconsidered in light of remaining responses. Only after fully completing this reappraisal should any temporary concession of unsolvability be entertained before continuing deductive work.

These steps emphasize maintaining an impartial perspective that resists overconfidence or the urge to force premature conclusions without definitively supported inferences.

Mastering POE in Practice

Consistently applying the POE process across a wide variety of materials and disciplines is key to truly optimizing this powerful reading strategy. With repetition, the logical framework of POE becomes second nature, nurturing intuition for recognizing patterns and deductive reasoning. This progression from initial application to instinctual proficiency requires dedicated long-term cultivation.

Scientific Concepts

POE proves invaluable for deciphering technical language and theories conveyed concisely within scientific journals, abstracts, or textbooks. Methodically analyzing neologisms and compound terminology against context enables comprehension of advanced fields like medicine, chemistry, or physics, even when presented tersely. Accumulating successful POE practice with science content builds specialized pattern recognition expertise applicable to new concepts emerging within the same discipline.

Foreign Language Acquisition

Utilizing POE's process of deductive elimination to contextualize unfamiliar vocabulary rapidly accelerates second language learning. Integrating POE into memorization strategies leverages structural clues to deduce cognates rather than passive translation alone. Repeated judicious

POE application makes language patterns intuitive, with education transferred to retain new lexicons longer-term.

Standardized Testing

POE preparation deserves focused time investment, as these skills directly impact performance. Working test questions under timed conditions simulate high-stakes settings. Recognizing flawed response patterns empowers eliminating implausible choices before guessing aimlessly. Pre-test practice applying POE methodology boosts testing confidence and competence.

While no field leaves context consistently sparse, certain disciplines particularly benefit from POE's nuanced deductive abilities. Legal documents eschew oversimplification, assuming readership comprehends intricate terminology contextually. POE develops this advanced comprehension capacity. Similarly, historical analyses reference figures and events sparsely explained, inviting readers to fill contextual gaps inferentially.

Beyond academic domains, POE readily transfers to professional contexts. Medical professionals apply it to diagnosing patients amid imperfect information. Paralegals utilize logical inferences to understand complex legislation from precedents. POE tutors intuitive comprehension from hints rather than pedantic explanations, empowering ambitious learners across disciplines. Most profoundly, it cultivates long-term independent critical thinking and problem-solving instincts applicable throughout life.

Poetry: Keeping you cool

Within the broad realm of creative expression, poetry occupies a tranquil space that nourishes both mind and spirit. Conveying complex ideas through ingeniously simple language, poems hold the power to soothe life's turbulence in readers of all backgrounds. This writing explores poetry's therapeutic effect and techniques for incorporating its study into a relaxing self-care routine. Sections provide guidelines for selecting accessible works reflecting personal interests and approaches to fully immersing in poetic ambiguity. With regular practice perceiving poems' nuanced worldviews, stress melts as higher states of focus take hold. In trying times, keeping poetry close easily maintains composure.

Finding Relatable Works

To reap calming benefits, start a personalized poetry collection reflecting personal passions. Browse anthologies previewing various styles until a thematic niche resonates. If nature enthuses, seek poets describing landscapes. Prefer history? Biographical poems bring distant eras near. Sports fans find the competition's spirit metaphorically conveyed. Given poetry's diversity, all may locate inspirations suiting temperaments. Build familiarity first with simpler, lyrical poems communicating through imagery before complex forms requiring deeper study. Accessible introductions through favorite styles or authors nurture continued exploration.

Learning Through Listening

Audio recordings complement visual apprehension, awakening imagery through a secondary sensory channel. Hearing cadences, pauses, and intonations brings words alive differently than silent reading alone. Public radio stations regularly air poetry programs. Download podcasts like "The Slowdown," presenting works accompanied by ambient scores. Poets.org supplies narrated selections; standardized testing sometimes omits for brevity. Stay away from analyses interrupting organic flow; focus instead on internalizing language's subtle music unaided as intended. Auditory immersion cultivates nuanced perspective.

Find Peace in Ambiguity

Unlike prose explicitly relaying concrete plots, poetry intentionally leaves much unstated. Rather than frustrating comprehension, embracing this obscurity breeds calm through subjective interpretation. Poems welcome diverse valid understandings, refusing any definitive solving. Their ambiguity invites reflective wandering without pressure to arrive at single right answers demanding cures for unrest lie elsewhere than logic. Surrendering to suggestive symbolism transfers control, paradoxically empowering through acceptance that mysteries persist untamed within life's framed beauty.

Savoring Imagery and Rhythm

Literary devices like metaphor, personification, and repetition weave music intrinsically relaxing. Visualizing comparisons concretely stimulates the imagination while rhythm's pulse soothes frazzled nerves and occupied minds. Poems utilize repetition sparingly for accentuated effect; with each revisiting of a metaphoric image or reverberating line, comprehension deepens while tension dissolves. Savor language's blending flavors without hurry, paying detailed attention to every layered nuance transpiring throughout works gradually unveiled. Staying present with each discovery replenishes depleted reserves.

Harmonizing Mind and Body

The relaxation poetry cultivates intensifies through multisensory engagement. Read selections aloud for a full-bodied experience of cadenced syllables. Notice how vocal tones shade implications. Scan visual line breaks and stanzas complementing phrasing. Pair readings with calming activities like gardening, origami, or sketching to simultaneously soothe the body through methodical motions. Beyond solitary practice, sharing poems with compassionate listeners multiplies stress-relief as caring dialogue emerges over shared affections. Poetic communion harmonizes individuals and communities through the elevation of a peaceful spirit available to revitalize all.

Sentence Function: Understanding Why Sentences Are Included

Effective communication relies on intent and structure within written language. As the fundamental unit conveying complete thoughts, the sentence plays a pivotal yet nuanced role in composition. Beyond grammatical rules, sentences fulfill specific communicative functions driving the progression and comprehension of ideas. This essay explores the principal reasons authors include particular sentences within a unified work. Sections outline major functional categories sentences assume based on the logical relationships and purposeful role each plays at the local and global level. With a reinforced understanding of function influencing formation, writers gain finesse crafting cohesive, impactful statements aligned to intentionally further meaningful expression.

Subject Sentences

As the backbone relaying core concepts, subject sentences introduce key topics, framing the ensuing discussion. They perform a baseline function establishing thematic parameters for subsequent sentences elaborating on the declared subject.

Importance of Subject Sentences

Subject sentences are fundamentally important building blocks that serve several critical purposes in strengthening written work.

Establish Direction and Focus

By directly announcing the core topic or concept, subject lines give readers a clear sense of the paragraph's intended subject matter. This removes ambiguity and channels attention productively.

Provide a Framework for elaboration.

Providing an initial statement of the subject creates a thematic framework for subsequent sentences to expand upon and add context to. It establishes parameters that unite details under a common subject.

Guide Coherent Navigation

Directly announcing the subject helps orientation within the discussion, allowing readers to follow the progression of ideas. It forms a cognitive roadmap for smoothly transitioning between various supporting notions.

Reinforce Cohesion

The regular restatement of subjects through strategic placement helps maintain the thread and strengthen bonds between concepts across sentences and paragraphs. It enhances flow and prevents disjointedness.

Encourage Retention

Clearly, introducing principles in subject sentences aids the retention of significant ideas. Leaving concepts only implicit risks losing the reader's grasp of discussion parameters.

Simplify Composition

Directly addressing the subject simplifies composition by clarifying intent and focus for developing detail sentences. Indirect or vague approaches complicate both writing and reading comprehension.

Signal Paragraph Structure

Readers immediately recognize the subject sentence as the launching point and central pillar for each unit of discussion. This reassures comprehension of the paragraph framework.

Convey Importance

By definition, the subject is the most essential element – directing attention to it signals its prominence relative to supporting details.

Types of Subject Sentences

Basic Subject Sentences

The most straightforward subject sentences clearly and concisely introduce the central subject or topic of the paragraph in a simple, direct statement. They lay the groundwork for additional detail or explanation.

Complex Subject Sentences

Longer, more syntactically intricate subject sentences can be used to draw in the reader with more compelling language or preliminarily present multiple interrelated facets of the subject matter.

Implied Subject Sentences

At times, particularly in highly cohesive writing, the subject may be implicitly rather than expressly stated through context clues, trusting the reader to discern the underlying topic from related content.

Effective Placement of Subject Sentences

Leading Paragraphs

Placing subject sentences at the start brings immediate focus and direction before elaboration begins. This classical format reassures clarity.

Concluding Placement

Ending paragraphs on the subject line provides cognitive bookends encouraging retention of the central subject in conclusion.

Strategic Internal Placement

Judicious mid-paragraph subject reminders prevent comprehension lapses across complex developing discussions.

Detail Sentences

Providing supporting facts, examples, descriptions, and clarifications, detail sentences flesh out subjects simply presented. They perform an explanatory function expanding upon foundational statements for enriched reader understanding.

Types of Detail Sentences

Fact-Based Detail Sentences

Details strengthening assertions with concrete facts aid persuasiveness. Statistics, data, and physical evidence add credibility.

Example-Driven Detail Sentences

Illustrations through specific examples bring intangible ideas to life vividly for readers to visualize.

Descriptive Detail Sentences

Elaborative descriptions of scenarios, people, places, and concepts nourish imaginative understanding beyond bare facts.

The Role of Detail Sentences

Support and Elaborate the Subject

Details directly relate to the central subject, providing explanatory context sans digression.

Target Significant Elements

Varying specific details emphasizes different vital aspects for a well-rounded perspective.

Engage Multiple Senses

Multi-sensory details heighten engagement through tangible mental images and fuller richness.

Effective Placement of Detail Sentences

Distributed Organization

Interweaving details methodically strengthens the subject on multiple levels across its discussion.

periodic Summarization

Brief restatements of the subject accompanied by cumulative salient details maintain clarity.

Logical Progression

Sequencing details to logically flow from general to specific supports cohesive argumentation.

Importance of Detail Sentences

Detail sentences serve several important purposes that enhance writing:

Flesh Out the Subject

Providing descriptive context and specific instances surrounding the subject develops a deeper, fuller understanding for readers beyond surface-level statements.

Strengthen Arguments

Well-chosen facts, statistics, examples, and details lend concrete evidence and Credibility to assertions being made, making the case more persuasive.

Engage Readers

Multisensory details enliven discourse through vivid imagery and scenarios that immerse readers rather than passive delivery of concepts. This boosts engagement and retention.

Expand Horizons

Elaborative clarification of various facets and implications of the subject matter nurtures nuanced comprehension by revealing new dimensions and viewpoints.

Guide Comprehension

Methodically unfolding subject matter gradually builds understanding as readers follow a logically sequenced exposition informed every step of the way.

Retain Focus

Periodically restating the core subject while providing explanatory details maintains orientation and ensures all content remains anchored to the primary subject.

Enhance Cohesion

Coordinating language linking details back to the subject sentence ties all components together cohesively into a unified, interconnected discussion.

Personalize Message

Illustrating intangible ideas with personalized, concrete instances has a more persuasive impact than dry facts alone by appealing to human relatability.

Leave Imprint

Illustrative details create unforgettable mental pictures that last beyond the initial reading to facilitate recall and application of significant subject matter.

Transition Sentences

Guiding discourse progression cohesively, transition sentences perform a linking function between independent concepts. They redirect readers' focus by signaling topic shifts and bridging subject changes.

The Role of Transition Sentences

Maintain Flow

Transitions reassure coherence when progressing fundamentally distinct notions by demonstrating the logical connection between elements.

Signal Progression

Signaling shifts prepare readers for new information after the completion of the previous subject.

Forms of Transition Sentences

Internal Transitions

Connect aspects within a singular complex discussion through logical or sequential terms like "furthermore, "in addition."

Paragraph Transitions

Link entire units with phrases like "turning now too," "the next important point," and handling progression to new subjects.

Larger Discourse Transitions

Phrases like "having discussed X, we now move to Y" smoothly conduct discourse across broader divisions of content.

Effective Transition Placement

Beginning Transitions

Orient readers are starting new sections, indicating logical association to what was previously addressed.

Mid-point Transitions

Pacing shifts prevent lengthy discussions from becoming disconnected through intermittent signaling.

Concluding Transitions

Reinforce takeaways and foreshadow potential future work when finishing discrete sections.

Importance of Transition Sentences

Transition sentences serve several vital purposes in strengthening cohesion and readability within writing:

Guide Readers

They redirect focus and prepare readers for a new subject or shift, maintaining a logical flow between ideas.

Signal Progression

Transitions signal completion and direct progression, helping readers follow argument development across interrelated topics.

Ensure Coherence

By demonstrating connections between concepts, they reassure comprehension of a rational continuum versus disjointed declarations.

Prevent Abruptness

Gradual shifts are easier to follow than sudden drops into differing subjects without contextual preparation or links.

Pace Complexity

Within lengthy discussions managing multiple interconnected topics, transitions balance depth with readability.

Highlight Structure

Their strategic placement reassures understanding of how individual components interconnect and build sequentially.

Demonstrate Logical Thinking

Indicate the sensible conceptual relationships unifying distinct elements into a holistic framework or train of thought.

Emphasize Associated Topics

Linking topics draws attention to their relative significance within the overarching discussion or argument.

Leave Imprint

Signals for progression also cue retention of important bridge concepts taken between dissociated subject matters.

Cultivate Flow State

Smooth, guided transitions encourage engaged reading by maintaining clarity and immersion versus disjointed jumps.

Concluding Sentences

Wrapping up ideas fully and bringing discussion full circle, concluding sentences perform the vital bookending function of completing thoughts.

Forms of Concluding Sentences

Summative Conclusions

Directly restate the subject and main assertions plainly to imprint significant notions clearly.

Reflective Conclusions

Pose thought-provoking questions or perspectives drawing on what was examined to stimulate lingering consideration.

Transitional Conclusions

Suggest implications or directions for future work while wrapping up discrete sections.

The Roles of Concluding Sentences

Reinforce Takeaways

Well-crafted conclusions imprint enduring understanding by re-emphasizing crucial subject matter and inferences.

Tie off Threads

Reasserting subjects brings closure while reviewing the progression accomplished before turning to new discussions.

Stimulate Further Thought

Thoughtful conclusions leave cognitive imprints that prolong engaging with conveyed messages and meaning.

COMPREHENSIVE READING DRILL

Mastering reading is crucial for lifelong learning and competence across all disciplines. Beyond decoding words, true comprehension entails actively engaging with texts through questioning, visualizing, and drawing inferences. This process nurtures intellect while sparking creativity. Regular practice strengthens such higher-order processing. Comprehensive reading drills provide structured yet stimulating exercises, developing a nuanced understanding of fiction and nonfiction. This essay outlines effective techniques for implementing drills independently or in classroom settings. With diligent application, drills cultivate perspectives and wisdom accessible through absorbing diverse sources.

Before Reading

Preview texts by examining titles, headings, visuals, and opening/closing paragraphs. Make predictions while considering authors' intentions and cultural contexts. Generate questions to explore arising from previews. Outline expected content flow by paying close attention to structural cues and their anticipated relationships. Adjust pace and focus as needed according to text complexity, knowledge, and time availability. Relating previews to interests and prior knowledge engages schemas, facilitating insightful connections.

During Reading

Annotate copies by underlining significant quotations and marking vocabulary to research. Note page numbers for easy referencing. Write commentary analyzing varied components and how they interrelate. Express wonderings stemming from interpretations. Visualize by drawing representations of settings, characters, scientific phenomena, or processes described. Formulate more questions to resolve ambiguities. Re-read confusing parts until they comprehend fully. Periodically restate main ideas and relationships understood thus far. Flag pages benefit from future in-depth analysis.

After Reading

Re-examine annotations, notes, and diagrams taken to consolidate understanding. Revisit questions requiring refinement or leaving curiosity unquenched. Revise interpretations as needed based on discoveries made through diligent inspection. Determine messages, moral lessons, or applicable insights conveyed through rereading with a broader perspective. Research unfamiliar terminology and contexts, deepening knowledge through additional learning. Discuss readings with peers and experts, proposing interpretations for insightful debate. Finally, reflect upon personal enrichment experienced and how exposures may influence future thinking.

Summarizing Fiction

For narratives, outline character development journeys emphasizing motivations and transformations. Analyze how plot points relate through rising action, climax, and resolutions. Identify prevalent themes and supporting evidence within the work as a cohesive experience. Take note of authors' craft techniques like foreshadowing, symbolism and narrative point of view contributing to intended effects. Consider sociocultural relevancy and timeless implications through a broadened historic lens transcending initial contexts. Summarize holistically to demonstrate full comprehension of dynamics forming the integrated whole.

Summarizing Nonfiction

With informational pieces, systematically map out the logical flow of topics, subtopics, and supporting details as presented. Restate clearly-communicated purposes, central assertions and lines of reasoning advanced through evidence examined. Notice persuasive strategies crafting cogent arguments and making compelling cases. Critically evaluate sources cited and their credible role in reinforcing conclusions. Where applicable, explain how to apply edifying principles and implications to daily life practices. Always summarize nonfiction through an objective lens while maintaining clarity on positions assumed from authors' intentions.

Summarizing Graphic Formats

Graphic novels, diagrams, and visual texts benefit from summaries describing relationships conveyed nonverbally through symbolic depictions, design choices, and accompanying narratives. Note imagery emphasizing particular concepts and purposefully guiding emotions, impressions, or interpretations sought. Analyze how such works synthesize words and images to convey depth exceeding either modality alone. Specify integrated themes emerging across visual and linguistic components coherently fused. Discuss cultural and historical relevance transcending entertainment through sociological insight potentially attainable via inclusively representational styles.

Connecting to Self and Society

Generate reflective inquiries considering the impacts readings may have on broadening personal perspectives, stances, or endeavors. Note potential applications in education, career-building, or civic participation. Brainstorm further avenues for addressing societal issues constructively portrayed or alluded to given acquired awareness. Share enlightened stances and inspired proposals through respectful discussion, cultivating positive change. Revisit works periodically to assess ongoing resonance while witnessing own evolution sparked by enriched reservoirs of information and imagination amassed from conscientious immersion experiences.

Cultivating Comprehension

Regular practice synthesizing multiplicity into singularity through comprehensively summarizing diverse texts instills higher-order processing mechanics serving lifelong advantage. With mindful dedication to insightful drill routines focused on active involvement, appreciation for knowledge becomes contagious while capacity and eagerness for learning grows boundless—a testament to the boundary less human spirit so beautifully mirrored through every page.

RULES QUESTION

Rules play an important role in reading and writing activities. However, not all rules are equally suitable. Questioning rules constructively helps teachers and students determine relevance and identify areas for improvement. This essay outlines an approach for analyzing reading and writing rules through open-minded inquiry.

Question Purpose and Rationale

Questioning Contextual Fit

When evaluating a rule's contextual fit, teachers should thoughtfully analyze changes in:

- **Technology usage** - Do rules accounting for online/digital texts still apply?
- **Student demographics** - Are cultural representation and inclusion reflected?

- **Family dynamics** - Have home/community factors influencing learning shifted?
- **Academic expectations** - How do standards/assessments now differ from the past?
- **Individual circumstances** - What new medical/neurodivergent needs exist?

Rules ignoring modern realities risk becoming irrelevant or even detrimental to learning.

Effectiveness Evidence

To judge a rule's true practical impact, teachers can:

- Administer student surveys anonymously, querying reading attitudes, confidence, comprehension, preferences for flexibility, etc.
- Conduct focus groups to explore diverse stances and elicit constructive ideas.
- Compare assessment data between classes under altered reading rule frameworks to measure influence on achievement objectively.
- Note student questions/comments during reading to identify where rules support or disrupt engagement and meaning-making.
- Solicit parent feedback to gain insight into home reading dynamics with different rules.
- Review assignment quality across rule-based conditions.

Collaborating with colleagues and applying alternative approaches also enables evidence-based perspective exchanges for ongoing progress.

Questioning Writing Rules

Brainstorm Rule Alternatives

Generating alternatives allows for assessing additional options beyond the status quo. Teachers can:

1. Assign small groups to envision novel possibilities, inspiring peers
2. Display idea posters for voting to surface consensus favorites
3. Propose provisional adjustments in writing workshops for real-time feedback
4. Facilitate idea-sharing between classes or grade levels school-wide
5. Incorporate student suggestions into future pilot implementations

Solicit Student Perspectives

There are several effective ways for teachers to solicit insightful student perspectives on writing rules. One method is to conduct individual student interviews. Interviews allow teachers to explore a diverse range of opinions in a one-on-one setting. This comfortable environment may help students feel more willing to openly share their experiences and delicate feedback regarding rules. During interviews, teachers can pose open-ended questions and actively listen without interruption to gain a thorough understanding of each student's unique perspective. Administering anonymous open-ended surveys is another technique teachers can use. Surveys provide an opportunity for students to privately disclose any perceived barriers or supports related to current rules. This anonymity may encourage honest feedback.

Additional ways for teachers to gather qualitative student input include holding town hall-style forums or facilitating anonymous online feedback. Town hall discussions enable respectful debate among the entire class around various rule proposals under consideration. Debates can help surface diverse viewpoints collectively. Establishing an anonymous online feedback dropbox allows students to digitally submit comments without attribution. Similarly, teachers may consider allowing for optional virtual feedback sharing via private video or audio recordings. This gives students control over their anonymity while still valuing their voices. Employing varied input techniques aims to incorporate informed perspectives from as many students as possible into the decision-making process regarding writing rules.

Evaluate Authentic Applications

Teachers can review assignments using rubrics addressing:

- Incorporation of interests, experiences, or learning preferences
- Representation of cultural communities or traditions
- Integration of multimedia/digital literacy skills
- Opportunities for expression of identity or perspective
- Authenticity of tasks mirroring real-world writing purposes

Promote Cooperative Evolution

There are several key steps a teacher should take when piloting adjustments to writing rules. First, it is important to clearly communicate the rationale for any changes upfront in order to address student concerns before they begin. Collecting periodic feedback throughout the pilot program allows the teacher to determine if refinements need to be made mid-way.

Feedback will provide insights into how well adjustments are working based on student responses. It is also essential for the teacher to analyze assignment quality, completion rates, and student responses to quantitatively assess the impact of changes. Discussing progress regularly with participating classes provides opportunities for collaborative reflection. Once the assessment is complete, lessons learned from the pilot should be incorporated into wider implementation. Finally, even after full rollout, writing guidelines should continuously be revisited with student input to refine collaboratively as the impact of adjustments continues evolving over time.

Addressing Rule Adherence Challenges

Standardize Clear Communication

Standardizing clear communication is an important part of addressing rule adherence challenges. Teachers should take several steps to ensure students have a consistent understanding of all rules. An essential step is prominently displaying the rules in the classroom so that they are easily visible for reference throughout learning activities. It is also beneficial for teachers to regularly review rules with students and provide examples to help facilitate comprehension. Having rules both clearly posted on the wall as well as orally reviewed reinforces the message.

Providing each student with a written copy of the rules to share at home with parents or guardians keeps expectations consistent. Teachers must clarify any nuances in how rules should be properly interpreted differently for various types of assignments as well. Finally, soliciting feedback from students allows the teacher to identify and remedy areas of potential obscurity or lingering confusion regarding the rules. Taking a multifaceted approach helps minimize noncompliance due to uncertainty.

Cultivate Intrinsic Motivation

Cultivating intrinsic motivation is important for effective rule adherence. To foster inherent drive, teachers should engage students in rich discussions that connect writing rules to the development of lifelong learning skills. Having relevant rules facilitates students' personal growth. When students help craft rules, they feel more ownership over them. It is also beneficial for teachers to highlight how mastering rules provides empowerment and flexibility for different writing contexts in the future. Praising the depth of understanding that students demonstrate, rather than just compliance, encourages intrinsic drive as well. Framing assessments as opportunities for students to showcase their learning, rather than judgments of self-worth, supports intrinsic motivation too. Taking a holistic approach that emphasizes rules as tools for learning cultivates students' inherent interest in self-improvement.

Model Adaptability and Growth

In order to best address rule adherence, teachers must model adaptability and growth for their students. They should lead by example by showing openness to trial implementations of alternative ideas generated from continuous student feedback. It is important that teachers admit when their original perspectives change in light of new evidence brought to light through feedback. They must express dedication to ongoing progress in their own skills as both learners and educators. Teachers should celebrate behaviors like risk-taking, perseverance, and collaboration over any single perceived perfect solution. By recognizing the complexity and nuances involved in addressing the diverse realities and needs of all students, teachers can help foster an environment where rules evolve cooperatively. Modeling adaptability and a growth mindset encourage students to approach feedback and rule analysis responsibly.

This systematic and cooperative rules analysis supports relevance while celebrating student diversity, needs, and potential. Thoughtful questioning maintains instruction relevance through collaborative refinement.

PART III
STEADY
Master the Math Section

INTRODUCTION

The Math section is one of the most important components of the SAT exam. It makes up approximately 25% of your total SAT score and measures your ability to solve problems involving fundamental math concepts and applications. While math may come easy for some, for many students it presents a challenge that requires diligent practice and skill-building. However, with the right strategies and an organized, steady approach, you can significantly boost your Math score and achieve mastery of this section.

Part III of this SAT prep guide will outline the key steps to take to systematically strengthen your math abilities and gain the skills needed to excel on Test Day. Across multiple chapters, you will be equipped with test-taking techniques, exposed to the various math concepts assessed, and provided with comprehensive practice problems designed to build confidence and content knowledge. While math formulas and problem types may initially seem overwhelming, breaking the material into manageable parts will help you feel progressively more comfortable with each new topic. With steady, focused preparation over time using the methods in this guide, you can be well-positioned to tackle any math question the SAT throws at you.

Rather than employing a rushed "cram" approach in the weeks leading up to the exam, this section advocates for long-term, continual practice and review. Rush preparation often leads to temporary memorization without true understanding or retention of skills. The pace and structure outlined here mirror how the human brain best absorbs and retains new information – gradually, through spaced repetition and making connections between related concepts. Daily practice of 30-60 minutes, combined with a review of previously learned material, is a highly effective way to commit strategies and mathematical rules to long-term memory.

Keeping organized records of your progress, questions, and strengths/weaknesses along the way will also support personalized study.

Mastery is the goal, not just getting by with the minimum knowledge required to answer a handful of questions correctly. You want to have a full repertoire of math techniques and skills that serve you well throughout high school, college entrance exams, and beyond - not just on one SAT test date. Achieving genuine mastery is empowering because it provides confidence in your abilities, no matter the specific questions asked. It allows you to utilize time more efficiently during the actual exam by avoiding misreads or uncertainty. This section guides you systematically through the full range of math concepts assessed on the SAT to attain that level of comfort and competence.

While math classes in school move at a certain pace, it is important to adopt a self-paced study strategy that works best for your individual needs and schedule when prepping for the SAT. Some topics may require more focus than others based on your baseline abilities. Feel empowered to spend extra time solidifying weaker areas or skipping ahead briefly to something more interesting if motivated to learn faster. Frequent review and practice of previously learned material is still essential to long-term retention, no matter your pacing preferences. Listening to your needs and making slight adjustments to fit your learning style will help maximize engagement and results.

Don't forget that mindset plays a large role in math performance as well. In addition to technical skills, cultivate a growth mindset that views challenges as opportunities to develop new understanding rather than signs of inability. Celebrate small victories and progress along the way to stay motivated. Seek help from teachers, tutors, or online resources without hesitation when stuck instead of wasting valuable time struggling alone. Have confidence that with consistency and perseverance, your math competence can substantially improve over the months you dedicate to SAT preparation.

Now that you understand the value of a thorough, steady approach to truly mastering the math section material, it's time to get started! Up first is a refresher on the format and question types tested to help familiarize yourself with the exam structure. From there, subsequent chapters will move through math topics in a sensible sequence, from algebra to functions to geometry, providing examples, explanations, and ample practice problems at each stage. Stay focused yet flexible in your preparation, take breaks when needed, and consistently apply what you learn. By the time Test Day arrives, your math skills and test-taking strategy will be fully sharpened to earn your best possible score.

FUNDAMENTALS

The math section of the SAT aims to assess students' mastery of core math concepts through a variety of question formats. While the exam covers higher-level math, it is important to have a solid grounding in more basic mathematical principles, which provide the building blocks for complicated problems. This article will outline the fundamental math skills tested on the SAT through detailed explanations organized under relevant headings and subheadings. A strong grasp of these basics is essential for SAT success.

Numbers and Operations

Number sense and fluency with basic calculations underpin many SAT math questions. Students must be able to both identify the values of digits in numerals up to the millions place as well as quickly and accurately perform operations involving whole numbers, decimals, fractions and integers. Developing speed and accuracy with calculations is essential for earning maximum points, as multiple-choice questions often require computing numerous steps without the aid of a calculator.

Whole Numbers

Questions routinely require adding, subtracting, multiplying, and dividing multi-digit whole numbers without a calculator. Students must recognize the base-ten structure and place values up to the millions to efficiently solve problems. Regular practice with whole number operations will help strengthen fluency and endurance for on-test calculations. Word problems may also incorporate whole number computations, requiring test-takers to accurately translate written information into numeric expressions.

Decimals and Fractions

Problems deal with decimals to the thousandth place and compare the magnitude of decimals and fractions. Students must be able to convert between decimals and fractions, add, subtract, multiply, and divide fractions and decimals, and simplify fractional expressions. Skills like determining the common denominator to add or subtract fractions and canceling terms when dividing fractions are expected to be second nature for SAT success.

Integer Operations

Understanding addition, subtraction, multiplication, and division of integers is tested routinely, as is combining like terms and simplifying integer expressions and equations. Absolute value is also assessed. Mastering the basic properties of integer operations, such as keeping track of sign changes when multiplying or dividing integers, is foundational. Word problems may present real-world scenarios involving integers, requiring students to set up and solve equations accordingly. Regular practice with integers in isolation and in applied contexts strengthens familiarity with these fundamental concepts.

Order of Operations

Following the correct order of operations without grouping symbols (PEMDAS - Please Excuse My Dear Aunt Sally) is vital to accurate calculation. Examples clarify precedences within expressions. Questions may include complicated expressions containing multiple operations that must be performed in the proper sequence to arrive at the correct solution. Students should make an order of operations second nature through consistent practice evaluating expressions step-by-step. Practicing on a calculator can help verify understanding and build confidence in applying PEMDAS. Common mistakes stem from careless errors in tracking exponentiations versus multiplication or division.

Ratios and Proportions

Examples require solving proportions, written as fractions equal to one another, as well as working with percentages. Converting customary and metric units using ratios is common. To set up and solve proportions successfully, test-takers must have mastery of fraction and decimal operations, as well as the cross-product property for determining if quantities are in the same proportion.

Algebra

Algebraic fluency is key on the SAT. Students must be prepared to simplify expressions, solve linear equations and systems, graph functions, and work with exponents and radicals. Comfort with algebraic manipulation is built through varied practice in translating word problems into mathematical representations and operations. Making mistakes in algebra often stems from careless errors, so students should double-check their steps.

Expressions

Manipulating numerical expressions with variables requires combining like terms, applying commutative, associative, and distributive properties, and factoring quadratic expressions. Questions may involve multistep simplifications requiring the strategic selection and application of several algebraic properties. Beyond field-specific skills, students must think cognitively about the overarching goal of an expression in order to effectively and efficiently simplify and manipulate algebraic expressions in various forms. Demonstrating this type of flexibility and higher-order thinking is an important part of evidence-based reasoning on the SAT.

Equations

One-step and multi-step equations involving one or two variables assessed linear, quadratic, radical, rational and absolute value equations. Systems of linear equations are also tested. Isolating the variable and maintaining equivalent equality across each step are essential skills for successfully solving routine equations. More challenging questions may require multiple operations to isolate complex expressions or solve compound equation types. Word problems translating between equations and contextual language reinforce algebraic reasoning and problem-solving abilities. Thorough practice with a variety of equation formats under time constraints prepares students for the pace and range of difficulty on test day.

Linear Functions

Concepts include determining rates of change from graphs or equations, finding the x- and y-intercepts, graphing lines by plotting points, and writing equations in slope-intercept form. Students must be facile, moving flexibly between graphical, numeric, and algebraic representations of linear functions. They may be given the graph of a line and asked to write the equation, or vice versa. Interpreting real-world scenarios as linear models and extracting meaning from quantified linear relationships is also assessed. Thorough practice translating linear functions from mixed formats builds the necessary fluency for demonstrating understanding through varied question styles on the SAT.

Exponents

Applying properties of exponents to simplify expressions involving positive, negative, and fractional exponents is tested extensively. Students must have committed to memory of the exponent rules, like how to distribute exponents when multiplying terms or combine like bases, in order to efficiently solve problems requiring multiple exponent steps. Careful attention to detail is important when working with exponents, as mistakes can easily arise from overlooked or misapplied properties.

Geometry

Various question types assess fundamental geometry topics such as points/lines, angle relationships, triangles, quadrilaterals, perimeter, area, volume, Pythagorean theorem, and coordinate geometry. Maneuvering flexibly between analytic proofs, constructions, and calculations contextualized in real-world scenarios indicates a well-rounded mastery of basic geometric principles.

Lines

Students must classify lines, write equations of parallel and perpendicular lines, find distances between points, and understand slopes. Questions may involve analyzing graphs of lines to deduce important properties like parallelism or orthogonality. The relationship between slope as the ratio rises/runs and its interpretation as the vertical and horizontal changes between points must be second nature. Putting concepts of slope, distances, and parallel/perpendicular categorization together lays the groundwork for success in coordinate geometry applications. Thorough practice of interweaving related line ideas strengthens flexible understanding.

Angle Relationships

Examples test complementary, supplementary, and vertical angle relationships as well as unknown angle measures. Demonstrating mastery involves more than memorization – it requires being able to analyze partial information about a geometric figure and apply the appropriate angle relationship to logically determine unknown values.

Triangles

Classifying triangles by side and angle measures and using triangle congruence and similarity principles is important. The triangle congruence criteria (SSS, SAS, ASA, and AAS), as well as calculating missing angles and identifying corresponding or proportional parts of similar triangles, are fundamental skills that must be recalled efficiently and applied accurately on SAT questions involving triangles.

Polygons

Naming quadrilaterals based on properties like equal sides and angles and finding missing attributes is assessed. Properties of rectangles, parallelograms, trapezoids, and rhombi come up frequently. Students must be able to logically work backward from given information about quadrilaterals to determine the classification or unknown values, choosing and chaining together concluding properties as needed to get the full picture.

Circles

Questions focus on diameter, radius, circumference, sectors, arcs, and applying formulas like the circumference formula 2πr. Students may be given a graphic of a circle or sector and asked to apply their understanding of these geometric relationships. Beyond recalling definitions and properties of circles, examinees must thoughtfully analyze diagrams, often under time pressure, to determine what specific parts are being referred to and apply the appropriate formula or reasoning. Measuring circle graphs and calculating segment measurements provides opportunities to showcase conceptual circle mastery.

Coordinate Geometry

Midpoint and distance formulas and graphing linear equations in the xy-plane are routinely emphasized. Students must be able to translate between linear equations and their graphical representations flexibly. Calculating geometric values like midpoints or distances between points presented numerically in the plane requires careful use of the formulas. More complex questions may involve the analysis of multiple linear graphs or geometric situations presented across mixed formats. Demonstrating versatility in coordinated algebraic and geometric reasoning is an important skill within this domain.

Perimeter and Area

Applying formulas to determine the perimeter and area of basic shapes like triangles, rectangles, and squares is fundamental. Extending skills to finding the circumference and area of circles provides more practice with geometry applications of numbers and algebraic formulas. Calculating perimeter and area combinations of attached shapes lays further groundwork.

Transformations

Basic rigid transformations like reflections, translations, and rotations develop students' spatial reasoning. Performing, identifying, and describing transformation sequences on geometric figures shows how congruence is preserved and lays the groundwork for understanding symmetries. This relates directly to essential geometry-proof skills as well.

ALGEBRA FUNDAMENTALS & STRATEGIES

For many students, algebra represents the gateway subject that either opens the door to higher levels of math and science or spells doom for their academic pursuits. Its symbolic language of variables, expressions, and equations seems foreign and impenetrable compared to the concrete arithmetic of years past. However, with the right mindset and methods, anyone can crack the algebra code and reach new heights in their mathematical journey.

Algebra is often seen as a complex, tangled web rather than a systematically solvable puzzle. But like any code, it has patterns, structures, and logical rules just waiting to be uncovered. The key is demystifying the subject piece by piece rather than viewing it as an overwhelming whole. With strategic practice, even the most intimidating problems are broken down into recognizable steps that can each be decoded methodically.

It also helps to understand that algebra is not just abstract symbols on paper but a way to represent and solve real-world scenarios. Equations model situations we encounter daily, from comparative shopping to traveling distances to investment growth. Making these tangible connections reinforces learning and builds confidence in one's ability to navigate algebraic situations.

This is where strategic techniques become invaluable - like breaking problems into smaller sub-problems, working examples backward, and estimating results before crunching numbers. Such approaches help organize the complexity into simpler cycles that can be analyzed and conquered step-by-step. With diligent effort spent cracking the system's inner workings, algebraic mastery is there for the taking.

This guide provides the code-cracking keys to algebra success: systematic methods, worked examples, and mindset shifts to unlock mathematics' most cryptic code once and for all. The algebraic mysteries hiding inside no longer need to be an insurmountable barricade - with the right tools and approach, anyone can crack the code.

Variables, Expressions & Equations

Contextualized Input Variables

Digital questions present algebraic terms within real-world contexts like word problems or diagrams. Input variables may represent amounts, speeds, prices, etc. Careful consideration of each variable's meaning rather than rote symbolism ensures correct responses update scenarios logically.

For example, a question about mixing solutions asks for amounts of ingredients (x, y) added. Students inputting randomly versus understanding variable definitions risks nonsensical results. Comprehension strengthens conceptual grounding.

Interactive Expression Manipulation

Rather than writing steps, online users directly operate on expressions through tools like "combine like terms." This allows checking work visually, reinforcing relationships between operational properties.

For example, combining 3x + 2x into 5x verifies the procedure without writing. Students see patterns rather than strictly following remembered rules, deepening conceptual connections.

Dynamic Equation Solutions

Digital equations update immediately when solving for variables interactively versus through written arithmetic. Correctly using tools like "isolate variable" directly demonstrates understanding rather than procedural skills alone.

For example, solving 2x + 3 = 5 for x visually confirms the solution x = 2 through direct manipulation rather than isolated steps. This reinforces mastery of the underlying logic powering algorithmic thinking.

Basic Equation Solving

Strategic Tool Usage

Digital solvers provide functions to isolate variables interactively rather than through written steps. The optimal strategy relies on discerning which tool(s) appropriately manipulate a given expression.

Solving Simple Equations

When solving an equation like 2x + 3 = 5, carefully considering the options shows that "isolate variable" most directly solves for x. Other choices require extra, unnecessary steps. Strategic discernment streamlines problems.

Solving Multi-Step Equations

A more complex equation like 5x − 2 = 3x + 7 demands strategic chaining of tools. First, using "subtract 3x from both sides" followed by "isolate variable x" solves the problem most efficiently on screen. Flexible thinking determines the optimal sequence.

Solving Polynomial Equations

To isolate variables in polynomial equations like x^2 − 4x + 3 = 0 requires factorizing first using tools like "factorize." Once factored to (x−1)(x−3) = 0, variables can be isolated straightforwardly. Strategic selection of factorization before isolation demonstrates strong conceptual understanding.

Avoiding Superfluous Steps

Functions exist to both isolate variables and manipulate expressions, so discernment avoids redundant steps. For example, on a simple problem like x + 3 = 7, directly using "isolate variable x" solves immediately without first unnecessarily using "subtract 3 from both sides". Strategic tool sequence streamlines efficient solutions.

Multi-Step Problem Solving

More involved equations require combining tools logically, demonstrating a strong grasp of conceptual underpinnings for each operational property.

Solving Equations with Two Variables

Equations like 3x + 5 = 2x − 1 involve manipulating both variables. Conceptual understanding dictates the proper order: first using "subtract 2x from both sides," which isolates the x terms, and then "isolate variable" to solve for x. The strategic sequencing demonstrates mastery.

Solving Polynomial Equations

More complex polynomials like x^2 + 5x + 6 = 0 require factorizing (x + 3)(x + 2) before setting individually factored terms equal to 0 can isolate solutions. The appropriate chaining of "factorize" and then "set equal to 0" functionality solves these types of multi-step problems methodically.

Solving Rational Equations

Rational expressions like (3x − 1) / (2x − 5) = 2 involve intentionally manipulating the given tools. A strategist may first opt to "clear denominators" to get a common denominator, then "isolate the variable." Carefully considering each step builds flexibility over rote responses.

Using Multiple Tools Concurrently

Some problems like 3x + 2(x − 5) = 7 necessitate using tools in tandem. Here, first using "distribute" followed by "subtract 2x" and then "isolate variable x" chains tools logically to a solution. Juggling handles underscores a strong conceptual grasp.

Meticulous Conceptual Application

Success involves precisely applying operational properties through digital functions, not mindlessly clicking. Thoughtful consideration of how each tool manipulates expressions/equations methodically solves multi-step challenges on screen.

Expression Manipulation

Functions like "factorize" or "simplify" prepare students to easily solve polynomials, rational expressions and other abstract equation types interactively.

Factoring Polynomial Expressions

Functions such as "factorize" allow students to rewrite expressions like $x2 - 4$, $x3 - 8x$, or $x4 - 16x2 + 64$ interactively through factoring patterns. For example, factoring $x2 - 4$ to $(x - 2)(x + 2)$ visually verifies factorization rules rather than relying on rote memorization. This reinforces conceptual understanding of factoring patterns.

Combining Like Terms

The "combine like terms" tool permits interactively collecting terms with the same variables and exponents, such as combining $3x + 2x + 5x$ into $10x$. Students see the outcomes of applying properties directly rather than through isolated written steps, strengthening the relationships between expressions.

Expanding Factored Forms

To move between factored and expanded forms, functions like "expand" allow visually verifying the expansion of $(x - 2)(x + 3)$ to $x2 + x - 6$ directly. This reinforces the inverse nature of factoring and expanding polynomial expressions on a conceptual level through technology.

Applying Properties Logically

More complex examples like applying the difference of squares identity to rewrite $x4 - 16$ as $(x2)2 - (4)2$ and then using "factorize" showcase flexibility in stringing together logical expression manipulation through strategic keyboard functionality.

Reinforcing Conceptual Mastery

Rather than following rote procedures, these tools reinforce students' familiarity with expression properties through experimentation in a just-in-time manner based on problem needs. The contextual application strengthens flexible, versatile thinking over isolated technical skills.

Concept before Calculation

The digital interface focuses on discerning a problem's structure and strategically selecting the sequence of tools needed to manipulate expressions and solve equations conceptually. This showcases the flexible application of principles rather than strictly calculating step-by-step.

Reinforcing Relationships

Functions strengthen connections between foundational number properties, operations, factors, expressions, and equations on an as-needed, problem-dependent basis. This dynamic, conceptual learning replaces detached memorization of isolated techniques.

Promoting Adaptability

While core topics remain constant, technology encourages comfort in applying conceptual understanding to various situations immediately through interactive experimentation. This cultivates flexibility over hyper-focus on rigid procedures alone.

Emphasizing Pattern Recognition

Digital problems emphasize discerning overarching structures or patterns to strategize suitable tool sequences rather than surface concerns like showing calculation work. This develops higher-level thinking habits.

avoiding Rote Responding

By promoting curiosity through dynamic applications, interactive formats circumvent simplistic memorization-based responses in favor of confident, original reasoning based on established foundations. Careful consideration precedes calculated solutions.

Fostering Independent Mastery

The online emphasis on flexible, insightful problem-solving transfers classroom expertise directly to independent, lifelong competence, navigating new quantitative scenarios conceptually through technology.

FUNCTIONS & GRAPHING

While core function properties remain the same, digital equations graphically react to input changes instantly. Experiencing the dynamic relationship between tables, rules, and graphs strengthens students' functional reasoning abilities. The strategy involves grasping patterns rather than memorizing rote steps, allowing extrapolation to increasingly complex examples. Learning functional structure transfers more effectively online through active experimentation beyond passive exposure.

Interactive Graphing

Digital graphing tools allow dragging axes, inputs, or plotting points to instantly observe output and graphical changes. This active exploration reinforces input/output relationships over passive absorption.

For example, dragging the (x,y) point on a graph of $y=x^2$ visually traces the parabola's path, strengthening conceptual understanding of quadratic behavior.

Understanding Functional Properties

Subtle changes to linear, quadratic, cubic, and other function rules and their tabular/graphical representations strengthen pattern recognition abilities.

For example, adjusting the rate of change or y-intercept for a line of best fit solidifies the meaning of the slope and y-intercept values.

Extrapolating Familiar Concepts

Deepening exposure to functions through varied online forms prepares students to confidently transfer understanding.

Experimenting with transformations like stretching/shrinking graphs of y=x informs an intuitive grasp of modifying coefficients within unfamiliar function families.

Bridging Representations

Fluidly interpreting graphs, tables, and equations develops multi-faceted functional thinking beyond any single view.

Relating exponential growth patterns in context to $y=ab^x$ forms and their graphical shapes strengthens multi-representational expertise.

Systems of Equations

The digital interface permits exploring systems graphically through immediate Cartesian plane updates or algebraically via symbol manipulation. Strong examinees combine methods, leveraging physical representations to confirm symbolic solutions. Under time constraints, leveraging provided tools optimally requires conceptual understanding rather than surface focus on isolated techniques. Technology reinforces higher-level system thinking.

Strategic Symbolic Solving

While graphing engages visualization, symbolic methods strategically eliminate variables, showing a strong conceptual grasp.

For example, manipulating 2x + 3y = 6 and x − y = 0 algebraically to isolate x and y strategically combines elimination and substitution to solve the system.

Applying Elimination Methodically

Systems of equations explicitly demand strategizing the logical elimination of variables to isolate solutions. Carefully manipulating equivalencies combines addition/subtraction with distribution to systematically eliminate one variable.

For example, when solving 2x + 3y = 6 and x − y = 0, strategic addition combines the equations, eliminating y terms to directly solve for x, then back substituting to find y isolates the solution point.

Introducing Substitution Deliberately

More complex systems necessitate elimination followed by intelligent back-substitution of a known value. The ordered process strengthens flexible thinking over rigid responding.

The example above finds x = 2 first through elimination. Then, substituting x = 2 into either original equation (x − y = 0 | 2 − y = 0) and solving for y isolates both variables x = 2, y = 2.

Assessing Conceptual Mastery

Rather than following rote steps, the symbolic approach emphasis conceptual comprehension of variable elimination and substitution to methodically manipulate multiple equivalencies strategically towards a solution.

Integrated Approaches

Strong examinees triangulate information, using graphical hints to identify promising algebraic steps or verify symbolic solutions on the coordinate plane.

For example, isolating x y terms and inspecting graphs of x = −1, y = 2 lines confirms (−1, 2) solves the system of 2x + y = 3, x − 2y = −4 both visually and symbolically.

Leveraging Graphical Insights Strategically

A system's graph provides clues to identify promising variable combinations for elimination/substitution algebraically. Discerning intersecting lines' graphs verifies symbolic solutions.

For the system 2x + y = 3, x − 2y = −4, isolating x = −1 and y = 2 through strategic methods and confirming the (−1,2) point satisfies both graphed lines reinforces the integrated nature of graphical and algebraic reasoning.

Validating Symbolic Work Visually

Upon finding symbolic solutions, examinees demonstrate understanding by verifying solutions satisfy the system's defining equations when viewed graphically through coordinate mapping.

For example, substituting the point (-1, 2) back into 2x + y = 3 verifies it satisfies the first equation when plotting to ensure the symbolic solution is correct.

Cross-referencing Representations

Fluidly connecting graphical, tabular, and algebraic representations of systems cultivate the facility to navigate multi-dimensional solution processes beyond surface skills in any one view.

Triangulating information through strategic cross-referencing of representations strengthens higher-order competence, flexibly solving systems through an integrated conceptual grasp.

Systematic Treatment

Approaching systems as patterned problems strengthens transfer rather than memorization of the rote process. Interactive consideration of systems conceptually optimizes multiple-choice time constraints.

Recognizing Underlying Structures

Systems adhere to consistent elimination/substitution patterns irrespective of surface attributes. Discerning deep structural similarities prepares students to flexibly transfer conceptual understanding.

For example, viewing 2x + 3y = 5, x - 2y = 3, and 2x - y = 1 as variations unveil their shared characteristics for strategic algebraic manipulation.

Anticipating Diverse Forms

Practice interacting with graphically, parametrically, and mathematically posed system examples strengthens predictive abilities beyond isolated memorized formats.

For instance, identifying a system presented contextually in a word problem, procedurally in a multiple-choice question, or conceptually through an algebraic transformation enhances transfer potential.

Optimizing Strategic Selection

Strong test-takers consider multiple approaches yet select the most efficient path, balancing speed and insight for a given question. Interacting with systems conceptually supports optimal response.

For example, a graphically posed system may prompt symbolic solving for direct verification, while an algebraically complex system could leverage graphical hints before symbolic manipulation.

Developing Flexible Expertise

Exposure to purposely varied system scenarios cultivates independent, versatile problem-solving far surpassing rigid following of predetermined steps alone. This enhances long-term quantitative proficiency.

Statistics and Data Analysis

Conceptual understanding transfers from theoretical to applied domains through digital interpretation and graphing of authentic datasets. Strategically selecting from analysis options necessitates comprehension of the statistical processes behind each. A problem-solving orientation stresses sense-making over calculation mechanics. Technology strengthens examinees' ability to connect numerical evidence to real-world contexts.

Interpreting Authentic Data

Interactive visualization and manipulation of genuine sets reinforce connections between measures of center, spread, distributions, and contextual implications.

For example, strategically plotting and overlaying histograms transfers comprehension of normal curves beyond rote definitions.

Making Informed Inferences

Strong test-takers leverage multi-faceted analysis options to derive justifiable conclusions, not blindly select surface-level metrics.

Correlating scatterplots strategically consider trend strength before immediately choosing a best-fit equation or R-value interpretation.

Connecting Statistics to Contexts

Data speaks through human experiences, so strategic inquiry probes plausible real-world explanations beyond calculation.

Considering alternative hypotheses expands critical thinking by pondering what data constraints imply about a situation rather than fixating on P-values.

Developing Adaptive Expertise

Encountering novel statistical presentations requires strategically selecting analyses, not rigidly adhering to predetermined steps. This enhances transfer potential.

For example, strategically summarizing data presented sequentially or ranking/rating data not in table/graph form.

Nonroutine Problem Types

Less familiar quantitative situations cultivate adaptive thinking through interactive explorations. Breaking into logical sub-steps and intelligently leveraging all available digital supports establishes strategic flexibility crucial for continued mathematics success. The technology prevents procedural fixation, instead emphasizing conceptual bridges between problems as foundations for original reasoning. Digital innovations reinforce mathematical versatility when confronted with novel scenarios.

Fostering Curiosity Through Novelty

Atypical problems spark motivation by necessitating creative, persistence-fueled thinking untethered from memorized solutions. Technological scaffolds thus enhance intrinsic interest in mathematical discovery.

For example, interacting with geometric or patterning puzzles prompts visual/strategic inferences requiring coordinated synthesis of fractions, formulas, and reasoning supported by available digital tools.

Developing Adaptability habits

Breaking nonstandard questions into manageable cognitive sub-goals and then systematically recombining information establishes durable critical thinking processes resilient to ambiguity beyond inflexible step-following.

Probabilistic or logically deductive scenarios demand carefully sequencing clues across multiple representations while optimally choosing digital supports toward justified inferences or conclusions.

Cultivating Original Thinking

Constraints inspire insightful approaches by relying on conceptual bridges linking domains, not surface appearances alone. This transfers expertise to genuine innovation when conventional frameworks prove limited.

Controlling Test Anxiety

While digital presentation adds complexity, strategic users transform technology into an anxiety-reducing asset. Familiarity with interface functionality through reinforcement practice builds navigational confidence and focus on mathematics over operations. Metacognitive routines like self-monitoring or thinking aloud calm nerves by redirecting attention to strategic reasoning. With experience, online testing felt less daunting and more like an interactive learning experience.

Familiarity Breeds Comfort

Repeated low-stakes practice with the assessment interface, tools, and response methods allows students to automate non-content tasks through over-learning. This relieves cognitive load during actual testing.

For example, ample digital scavenger hunts or simulated assessments familiarize examinees with menu options, text boxes, drag-and-drop, etc., so the format doesn't induce panic.

Redirecting Wandering Minds

Metacognitive routines like thinking aloud, problem-solving steps, noting anxious thoughts, and refocusing on reasoning processes regulate intrusive worries.

Self-monitoring and catching off-task mental tangents redirect energy toward strategic problem-breaking and tool selection instead of self-doubt.

Preventing Procrastination

Setting mini-goals or time budgets for conceptual subsets instead of dwelling on whole questions encourages steady progress versus debilitating uncertainty.

Strategically self-quizzing using practice questions as mental breaks maintains stamina and confidence via momentum from tackling easier related problems.

Reframing Failure Mindsets

Success is a skill cultivated through view practice as risk-free exploration versus proof of worth. Reframing mistakes as learning evidence counters fear of imperfection.

Over time, examinees gain perspective, recasting test anxiety as surmountable through the diligent development of effective problem-solving habits.

Digital Adaptability

Beyond content knowledge, developing comfort with emergent delivery modes positioned students to adapt naturally to future innovations. Exercising critical thinking around provided tools fosters facility transferring between representations and tackling unusual situations methodically. With practice, digital platforms feel less restrictive and more like partners in problem-solving. Building this agility strengthens examinees' preparation for unforeseen interactive assessment advances and careers requiring technical dexterity.

Developing Technological Comfort and Flexibility

Repeated exposure to different interface designs, input/output options, and organizational structures helps students think beyond the surface features of any single platform. This installs flexible habits, allowing them to adapt smoothly to new innovations. Practicing with simulated digital exams using unfamiliar yet logically consistent workflows strengthens their ability to navigate change.

Exercising Robust Critical Thinking Skills

Thoughtfully evaluating the strengths, weaknesses, and appropriate uses of various digital tools fosters an inquiry-based mindset focused on extracting maximal value from available resources. This prepares students to transfer understanding between representations and strategically select devices best matching task needs. For example, thought experiments manipulate concepts across graphical, numerical, and abstract formats.

Viewing Partnership and Potential

Rather than resisting the unknown, students learn to view emerging technologies as aligned problem spaces requiring thoughtful coordination. In this mindset, innovations open up creative opportunities through strategic coordination between human reasoning and machine capabilities. Previous challenges then serve as proof of their capability to rise above limitations through evidence-driven solutions.

Preparing for an Unpredictably Evolving World

Instilling an adaptable, growth-oriented approach helps students navigate unforeseen situations with both technical facility and resilience. Developing this mastery now establishes robust critical thinking habits, empowering lifelong curiosity and learning needed to thrive in careers demanding flexibility for constant changes. Repeated practice cultivates long-term preparedness for an evolving world.

Effective Problem-Solving Strategies

Thoughtful strategic approaches tailored to problem structures ensure maximum success. Translating contexts, checking units, systematic multi-step logic, and spatial visualization bolster skills. Estimating, checking solutions, flexibility in choosing optimal methods, and persevering through challenges build proficiency. Nonroutine problems require creative connections and breaking into sub-pieces.

Translating Contexts Carefully

Reading word problems thoroughly and mapping relationships between stated and quantitative variables strategically frames mathematical models. This supports conceptual understanding. Carefully analyzing all provided information allows students to discern which details are relevant to building equations or expressions. They learn to strategically extract only the necessary quantitative relationships and units of measure rather than getting lost in an extraneous narrative context. This strategic translation of verbal descriptions into symbolic representations lays the groundwork for conceptualizing and solving the mathematical scenario at its heart. It allows students to confidently manipulate and solve the abstract problem modeled after accurately comprehending the meaningful contextual details.

Checking Units Deliberately

Strategic double-checking that calculations yield reasonable estimates in proper measurement systems prevents errors from inconsistent units. Carefully attending to the units specified in the original information allows students to verify that their final numerical solution is expressed in the expected units based on the context of the problem. This could reveal if a conversion step was mistakenly omitted. The vigilance around units cultivates careful attention to detail that is necessary for success in multistep problems.

Applying Step-by-Step Logic Methodically

Breaking problems into sequential, verifiable cognitive steps reinforces partial understanding at each stage rather than confusion from overwhelming holistic views. Methodically writing out the logical progression and rationale behind each individual calculation builds conceptual scaffolding. Students learn to take complex multistep challenges and break them down into bite-sized pieces they can manage cognitively, one step at a time. This sequential approach prevents getting stuck on portions further along if initial steps are misunderstood, and it reinforces foundations at each point of progress.

Exercising Spatial Skills Strategically

Visual diagrams, graphic representations, and virtual manipulatives strengthen connections for geometry concepts over rote memorization. Strategically reasoning with multiple representations, such as pictorial diagrams alongside symbolic expressions or quantitative word problems, helps solidify geometric relationships in a multilayered, interconnected way. This deepens conceptual understanding beyond superficial definitions. Students learn to leverage the visual sense as a tool to strengthen their intuitive grasp of spatial relationships and problem-solving capabilities.

Estimating before Calculating

Estimating before calculating solutions checks work and conceptual grasp rather than mindless calculations alone. Developing fluency in reasoning about quantitative relationships and magnitudes allows students to quickly generate preliminary benchmark values to use for sanity checks. Predicting ballpark figures lets students evaluate whether a full calculation is yielding a result that makes logical sense based on the context of the problem. This strategic estimating cultivates critical thinking habits for ongoing self-monitoring of mathematical progress and conceptual understanding throughout the problem-solving process. Instead of simply computing mechanically, students learn to continuously engage in higher-order thinking.

Choosing Efficient Methods Flexibly

Strong solvers consider alternatives yet select optimized paths, balancing speed, understanding, and accuracy for each scenario rather than rigid adherence to a single method. They learn to strategically determine which solution approach will yield a correct answer in the most expeditious and error-resistant manner, depending on the specific characteristics of the problem. This may involve selecting between analytic or graphical methods, using calculators judiciously to reduce computational errors, or leveraging alternative algebraic techniques that provide greater conceptual understanding. The ability to flexibly evaluate multiple strategies and optimize the method of solution reinforces broader mathematical competency rather than narrow memorization or repetition of a single approach. Students develop flexible problem-solving skills that will allow them to approach novel situations with quantitative reasoning and select appropriate methods to accurately solve problems efficiently.

Persisting through Novel Challenges

Persisting through novel challenges is an important problem-solving strategy. Non-routine problems that don't clearly map to memorized algorithms cultivate discovery and deep learning. They require systematically drawing on core mathematical concepts in new ways. To solve unfamiliar problems, students must break them down and recombine the familiar elements into original conceptual frameworks. This demands creative, persistent trial and error — reworking potential approaches through multiple iterations. Learning to embrace challenges fosters a growth mindset. Students understand setbacks as opportunities to sharpen their innovative thinking. With practice, they gain confidence in their ability to leverage fundamental principles in novel scenarios. While non-routine problems may take more time and effort, they help cement flexible reasoning skills for tackling any unforeseen issues in the future. The problems promote life-long learning habits.

FUNCTIONS AND GRAPHS

In mathematics, understanding how quantities relate to each other is fundamental. Functions and graphs provide a powerful toolkit for expressing and visualizing these relationships. This chapter delves into the fascinating world of functions and graphs, equipping you with the key concepts and tools to navigate this essential branch of mathematics.

Functions: The Rules of Transformation

A function, at its core, is a special kind of relationship between two sets of numbers. Imagine a machine that takes in one number (the input) and transforms it according to a set of rules to produce another number (the output). This transformation defines the function.

Formally, a function denoted by $f(x)$ assigns a unique output value, $f(x)$, to each input value, x, belonging to a specific set called the domain. The collection of all possible output values that the function can produce forms another set called the range.

For instance, consider the function f(x) = 2x + 3. Here, x is the input, and the function doubles it and adds 3. The domain of this function encompasses all real numbers, as any real number can be doubled, and 3 can be added to it. The range, however, consists of all numbers greater than or equal to 3 since doubling any real number and adding 3 will always yield a value greater than or equal to 3.

There are several ways to represent a function. Algebraic expressions like f(x) = 2x + 3, tables that list input-output pairs, and even verbal descriptions can define functions. However, the most powerful and intuitive way to visualize a function's behavior is through its graph.

Graphs: The Visual Language of Functions

Imagine a coordinate plane with a horizontal axis labeled x and a vertical axis labeled y. Each point on this plane represents an ordered pair (x, y), where x is the horizontal coordinate and y is the vertical coordinate. The graph of a function is a collection of all such points where the x-coordinate corresponds to the input value (x), and the y-coordinate represents the corresponding output value (f(x)).

To graph a function, we can follow these steps:

- **Identify the function's rule:** This could be an algebraic expression, a table, or a verbal description.
- **Assign input values:** Choose a range of input values (x-values) from the function's domain.
- **Calculate output values:** For each input value (x), evaluate the function's rule to determine the corresponding output value (f(x)).
- **Plot the points:** Plot each ordered pair (x, f(x)) on the coordinate plane.
- **Connect the points:** Depending on the function's behavior, you might connect the plotted points with a smooth curve, create discrete dots for specific data points, or use other visual representations.

By plotting these points and connecting them appropriately, we obtain a visual representation of the function's behavior. The graph reveals how the output changes as the input varies. It allows us to see patterns and trends and identify important features of the function, such as its intercepts, extrema (maximum or minimum points), and asymptotic behavior (how the function approaches infinity).

Different Types of Functions

The world of functions is vast and diverse, each type reflecting a distinct kind of relationship. Here, we delve into some of the most common types of functions:

- **Linear Functions:** These functions represent a proportional relationship between the input and output. Their graphs are straight lines with a constant slope that determines the rate of change. Positive slopes indicate a direct proportion (output increases as input increases), while negative slopes signify an inverse proportion (output decreases as input increases).
- **Quadratic Functions:** These functions are represented by expressions of the form $f(x) = ax^2 + bx + c$, where a, b, and c are constants. Their graphs are U-shaped parabolas that can open upwards (minimum point at the vertex) or downwards (maximum point at the vertex), depending on the value of the leading coefficient (a).
- **Exponential Functions:** These functions depict rapid growth or decay. Their graphs are always positive and either continuously increase (for positive bases greater than 1) or continuously decrease (for bases between 0 and 1). The rate of growth or decay is determined by the base of the exponent.
- **Periodic Functions:** These functions exhibit repeating patterns. Their graphs repeat themselves over a specific interval called the period. Common examples include sine and cosine functions, which are fundamental in trigonometry and wave analysis.

Understanding these basic function types equips you with a foundation to explore more complex relationships and model real-world phenomena.

Applications of Functions and Graphs

Functions and graphs are not merely abstract mathematical concepts; they are powerful tools with far-reaching applications in various fields. Their ability to model and analyze relationships makes them indispensable in science, engineering, economics, computer science, and even everyday life. Let's explore some compelling examples:

Motion and Kinematics:

Imagine analyzing the motion of a car. We can define a function where the input is time (t) and the output is the car's position (d(t)). The graph of this function would depict the car's movement over time. The slope of the graph at any point represents the car's instantaneous velocity (rate of change of position). This application is fundamental in physics, helping us understand projectile motion, freefall, and various other types of motion.

Projectile Motion and Trajectories:

When launching a rocket or firing a projectile, understanding its trajectory is crucial. Functions can model the relationship between the launch angle, initial velocity, and the projectile's height and distance traveled at any given time. By analyzing the graph of this function, engineers can optimize launch parameters to achieve desired targets.

Supply and Demand in Economics:

Economics heavily relies on functions to model the relationship between supply and demand for a particular good or service. The price (p) acts as the independent variable, while the quantity supplied (Qs) and quantity demanded (Qd) are dependent variables represented by functions. The intersection point of these two functions, the equilibrium point, determines the market price where supply and demand balance.

Circuit Analysis and Electrical Engineering:

The behavior of electrical circuits can be modeled using functions. Ohm's Law, which states that voltage (V) is directly proportional to current (I) with resistance (R) as the constant of proportionality, can be expressed as a function (V = IR). By analyzing graphs representing voltage and current relationships, engineers can design and analyze circuits for optimal performance.

Growth and Decay in Biology and Population Studies:

Functions are instrumental in modeling population growth and decay in various species. Population growth can be represented by functions that consider birth rates, death rates, and environmental factors. Analyzing the graph of such a function can predict population trends and inform conservation efforts in biology.

Optimizing Costs and Revenue in Business:

Businesses utilize functions to model costs associated with production (e.g., cost as a function of the number of units produced) and revenue generated by sales (e.g., revenue as a function of price). By analyzing these functions and their graphs, businesses can identify points of minimum cost or maximum revenue, allowing them to optimize pricing strategies and production levels for profitability.

Cryptography and Secure Communication:

Functions play a vital role in modern cryptography. Encryption algorithms rely on complex mathematical functions to transform messages into unreadable ciphertext. Decryption utilizes the inverse function to recover the original message. The security of these algorithms hinges on the complexity of the functions used, making them difficult to crack by unauthorized parties.

Computer Graphics and Animations:

The world of computer graphics relies heavily on functions to define shapes, curves, and movements. 3D modeling software uses mathematical functions to represent objects and their transformations. Animation techniques employ functions to control motion paths, creating the illusion of movement and life in computer-generated images.

Signal Processing and Wave Analysis:

Functions are fundamental in signal processing and wave analysis. Electrical signals, sound waves, and light waves can be modeled by functions like sine and cosine functions. By analyzing these functions and their graphs, engineers can extract information from these signals, enabling applications like noise cancellation, image compression, and data transmission.

Predictive Modeling and Machine Learning:

Machine learning algorithms utilize functions to learn from data and make predictions. These functions establish relationships between input features (e.g., customer demographics in marketing) and target variables (e.g., purchase likelihood). By analyzing vast datasets, these algorithms can learn complex functions, allowing them to make accurate predictions and recommendations in various domains.

ARITHMETIC

Arithmetic, the bedrock of mathematics, serves as our fundamental toolkit for manipulating numbers. It equips us with the essential skills to perform calculations, solve problems, and understand quantitative relationships in the world around us. This chapter delves into the captivating realm of arithmetic, exploring its core operations, properties, and applications in various contexts.

Numbers and Operations

The cornerstone of arithmetic lies in the concept of numbers. Numbers are abstract symbols that represent quantities and allow us to perform calculations. We encounter a vast number system encompassing natural numbers (counting numbers: 1, 2, 3, ...), whole numbers (natural numbers including 0), integers (whole numbers and their negatives: ..., -3, -2, -1, 0, 1, 2, 3, ...), rational numbers (numbers expressible as a fraction: 1/2, 3/4, -5/7, ...), real numbers (rational numbers and irrational numbers like pi ($\sqrt{2}$)), and complex numbers (numbers involving the imaginary unit "i").

While the number system provides the foundation, arithmetic operations empower us to manipulate these numbers. The four fundamental operations of arithmetic are:

- Addition: This operation combines two numbers to yield a single sum. It represents the act of joining quantities together (e.g., 3 apples + 2 apples = 5 apples).
- Subtraction: This operation finds the difference between two numbers. It signifies removing a quantity from another (e.g., 10 oranges - 4 oranges = 6 oranges).
- Multiplication: This operation represents the repeated addition of a number to itself. It signifies scaling a quantity by a certain factor (e.g., 3 x 4 = 12, which is equivalent to adding 4 three times).
- Division: This operation distributes a quantity (dividend) amongst a specified number of equal parts (divisor). It essentially asks, "how many times does the divisor fit into the dividend?" (e.g., 12 divided by 3 = 4, as 4 multiplied by 3 equals 12).

These basic operations serve as the building blocks for more complex mathematical endeavors.

Fundamentals of Addition and Subtraction

Adding and subtracting are fundamental skills used throughout mathematics. Here are some key points about these operations:

- Addition combines sets or amounts represented by the addition sign +
- Subtraction removes part of a quantity, represented by the subtraction sign -
- Both operations can be done with whole numbers, fractions, and decimals
- Related concepts include sums, differences, addends, minuends, subtrahends
- Properties that apply are commutative, associative, and identity laws

Mastering addition and subtraction requires memorizing basic number facts like sums to 10 or 20. Mental math strategies like compensation are also important for efficient calculation. Place value understanding further enhances precision with larger numbers.

Properties of Arithmetic Operations

Just as tools require understanding their properties for effective use, so too do arithmetic operations. These properties govern the interactions between numbers and ensure consistent results during calculations. Here are some key properties:

Commutative Property

This fundamental property of arithmetic operations applies to both addition and multiplication. It formalizes the intuitive understanding that rearranging the order of numbers being added or multiplied together does not change the end result.

In addition, the commutative property can be stated as a + b = b + a, where a and b represent any two addend numbers. No matter which addend is placed first or second in the expression, the sums will always be equivalent.

Similarly, when multiplying any two factors, a and b, the commutative property dictates that a x b = b x a. Multiplication results remain identical regardless of which factor is listed first as the multiplier versus second as the multiplicand.

Being able to flexibly understand numbers from both order perspectives streamlines addition and multiplication calculations significantly. It also helps verify solutions and catch transposition errors. The commutative property ultimately expresses the numerical concept that the order of counting or grouping items holds no bearing on the final total quantity arrived at.

Associative Property

This property expands on the ability to rearrange numbers by grouping operations applied within parentheses. It ensures predictable, orderly processing of arithmetic expressions involving multiple operations strung together.

Associativity allows addition or multiplication to be distributed in fragments over grouping symbols like parentheses without altering the final solution. For instance, when adding three addends, the associative property guarantees that (a + b) + c is equivalent to a + (b + c).

Similarly, it establishes that multiple multiplication expressions like (a x b) x c will yield the same value as a x (b x c). Being able to flexibly reassociate terms aids in simplifying complex expressions and checking work in a methodical fashion.

Distributive Property

This crucial algebraic property streamlines combining terms when one operation involves both addition and multiplication. It formally captures the intuition that multiplying an entire grouping distributes or spreads the multiplication across each term within.

For example, when multiplying a binomial expression like 2(x + 3), the distributive property allows expanding this to its equivalent form: 2x + 6. Here, the number 2 is distributed as a factor over the sum x + 3, multiplying each term individually.

More generally, for any numbers a, b, and c, the expression a(b + c) is equal to the distributed form ab + ac. This property greatly simplifies multiplying out polynomial and algebraic expressions into more manageable component terms.

Being able to systematically apply distribution in either direction follows rational step-by-step reasoning and forms the basis of advanced algebraic manipulation of linear and quadratic equations. It is a fundamental tool throughout mathematics.

Identity Property

This crucial property marks unique numerical identities that leave other values unchanged under addition or multiplication. It formalizes the essential role these identities play.

For example, in addition, the identity element is 0. By definition, adding 0 to any other number n yields the unchanged original number: n + 0 = n.

Multiplicatively, 1 serves as the identity. Multiplying any n by 1 does not alter its value: n × 1 = n.

Equipped with the identity elements 0 and 1, any number can be added to or multiplied by the identity without variation – it is unchanged or identical to the original operand.

This property underlies higher-level proofs and lays the groundwork for beginning algebraic equation solving using identities to eliminate terms. Its formal designation emphasizes the vital role these anchor points play across mathematics.

Inverse Property

The inverse property provides a formal definition of the logical concept of undoing or reversing a mathematical operation. It incorporates the intuitive understanding that for every function or process, there is an opposing transformation that precisely cancels out the original action.

In arithmetic, addition, and multiplication, each has a well-defined inverse operation. The inverse of addition is subtraction – meaning that adding a number and then subtracting it returns to the original value.

For any two numbers a and b, the inverse relationship is expressed as:

a + b = c (original)

c – b = a (inverse)

The inverse of multiplication is division. If two numbers are multiplied to obtain a product c, dividing c by one of the original factors precisely restores the other factor.

For factors a and b:

a × b = c

c / a = b

Higher math builds upon this property – derivatives provide inverses of integrals in calculus, logarithms undo exponents, and so on. It gives logical structure to "undoing" steps and verifies solutions.

More broadly, the inverse property demonstrates arithmetic's consistency by formalizing the notion that operations can systematically be reversed through their inverses. This renders the number system coherent and predictable in both directions of change.

Understanding these properties allows for efficient calculation and manipulation of expressions. They streamline problem-solving and ensure the accuracy of our computations.

Applications of Arithmetic in Daily Life

While often relegated to the realm of early education, arithmetic's influence extends far beyond the classroom. It serves as the fundamental language of numbers, empowering us to navigate the complexities of the real world. From the seemingly mundane tasks of daily life to the intricate calculations of advanced fields, arithmetic underpins countless professions and activities.

Budgeting, Banking, and Personal Finance:

Arithmetic forms the backbone of personal financial management. We utilize addition and subtraction to track income and expenses, calculate budgets, and compare prices. Multiplication comes into play when determining loan repayments, investment returns, or calculating interest rates. Even basic division helps us split bills amongst friends or figure out unit costs when shopping.

Processing Inventory, Shipments, and Transactions

In the world of business, arithmetic plays a vital role in managing inventory. Businesses rely on addition and subtraction to track stock levels, calculate reorder points, and fulfill customer orders. Multiplication helps determine the total cost of goods based on quantity and price, while division allows for calculating shipping costs per unit or determining profit margins. Every transaction, from a simple grocery store purchase to a complex international trade deal, hinges on accurate arithmetic calculations.

Cooking, Construction, Manufacturing, and Other Measurement Applications

From the precise measurements required in delicate pastries to the large-scale calculations needed for building a skyscraper, arithmetic reigns supreme in various measurement-centric fields. Bakers rely on precise ratios of ingredients (cups, grams) achieved through multiplication and division to ensure consistent results. Construction workers utilize complex arithmetic calculations involving geometry and trigonometry to determine angles, distances, and material requirements. Similarly, manufacturers employ arithmetic to control production processes, calculate material usage, and ensure product quality.

Medical Measurement, Dosing, and Record-Keeping

In the realm of healthcare, even a slight miscalculation can have significant consequences. Doctors and nurses rely on accurate measurements (weight, height, temperature) to diagnose and treat patients. Medication dosages are meticulously calculated using arithmetic, considering factors like patient weight, age, and medication potency. Medical records themselves are filled with quantitative data, requiring arithmetic for analysis and interpretation.

Engineering Design and Quality Control:

The marvels of modern engineering, from towering bridges to sleek smartphones, all owe a debt to arithmetic. Engineers utilize complex calculations involving geometry, trigonometry, and calculus (built upon a foundation of arithmetic) to design structures, analyze stresses, and ensure functionality. Quality control measures in manufacturing also rely heavily on arithmetic for measurements, tolerance checks, and statistical analysis.

Data Analysis, Sampling, and Survey Work:

The world runs on data, and arithmetic serves as the key to unlocking its secrets. Data analysts use various statistical techniques (rooted in arithmetic) to identify trends, correlations, and patterns within vast datasets. When conducting surveys, sample sizes are determined using arithmetic to ensure representative data. Even the interpretation of percentages and averages, fundamental to data analysis, relies on a solid understanding of arithmetic principles.

A Stepping Stone to Higher Mathematics and Sciences:

While arithmetic forms the foundation, its influence extends beyond basic calculations. Geometry, trigonometry, algebra, and calculus, the cornerstones of higher mathematics and sciences, all build upon the foundation established by arithmetic. Mastering arithmetic concepts empowers individuals to delve deeper into these advanced fields, further unlocking the secrets of the universe and pushing the boundaries of human knowledge.

GEOMETRY AND TRIGONOMETRY

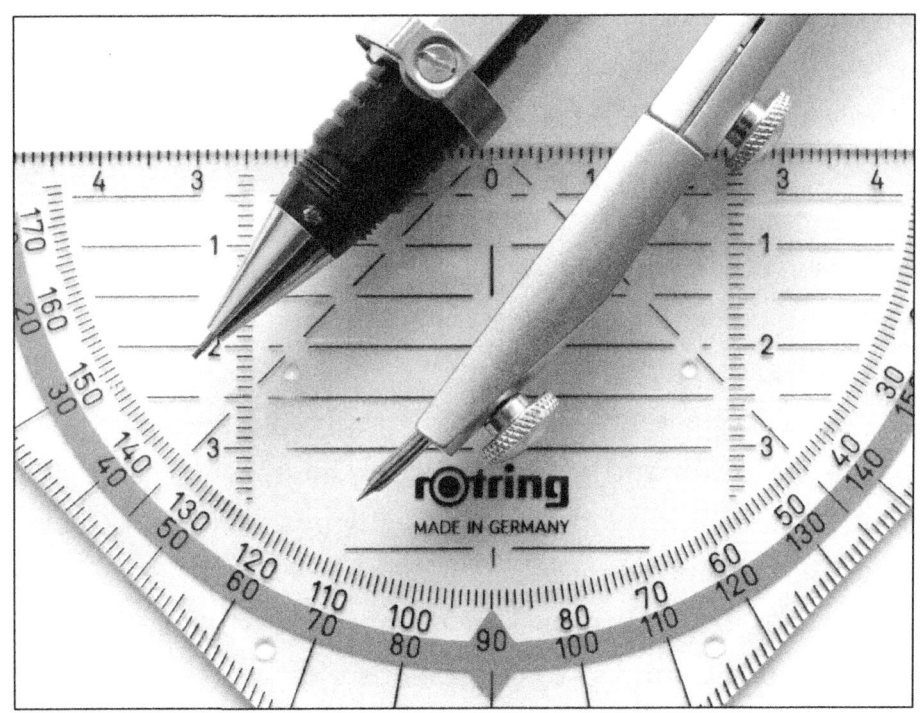

Geometry and trigonometry form the mathematical building blocks to describe properties of space, lines, angles, and shapes. This essay will provide a comprehensive exploration of key concepts from both geometrical and trigonometric domains. It will explain fundamental objects like points, lines, and angles, as well as transformations such as rotations, reflections, and translations. Additionally, it will delve into trigonometric functions, identities, and their geometric relevance through right triangles and coordinate systems. The goal is to equip readers with a solid conceptual foundation of these interrelated mathematical disciplines.

Geometry

The word geometry comes from Greek roots meaning "earth" and "measurement," as many of geometry's properties were first studied through land surveying. Some basic terms from geometry include:

Planes: A plane spans infinitely in two dimensions formed by three non-collinear points. These define a geometric space.

- Points: Points are considered to have no size or dimension; they represent a specific location in space. Imagine the tip of a sharpened pencil; it represents a point in space with no width or length.
- Lines: Lines are one-dimensional objects that extend infinitely in both directions. They have no width or thickness but represent a straight path. Imagine stretching a taut string infinitely; that would represent a line.
- Angles: Angles are formed by the intersection of two rays (parts of lines extending infinitely in one direction). The measure of an angle indicates how much the two rays diverge from each other, typically expressed in degrees (°) or radians (π radians = 180°). Imagine opening a pair of scissors; the angle between the two blades increases as you open them wider.
- Shapes: Fundamental shapes include line segments formed by two points, rays emanating from a point, and angles between intersecting lines. Polygons come in various sides, like triangles, quadrilaterals, pentagons, and so on. Circles are defined by points equidistant from the center.
- Transformations: Isometries preserve distances and angles while changing the positions of objects. **Examples** are translations sliding objects, rotations turning them, and reflections flipping over lines. Scaling uniformly enlarges or shrinks without changing shape.
- Congruence and Similarity: Figures are congruent if corresponding angles and sides are equal, while similar shapes maintain the same angles but may have different side lengths.
- Constructions: Geometry proves theorems by leveraging the compass, straightedge, and inventions. Postulates are basic assumptions like the existence of a line through two points. Proofs use logic to derive non-obvious results from these.
- Coordinate Geometry: Cartesian planes plot geometric objects in two or three dimensions using ordered pairs of real numbers. This connects algebra and geometry through linear equations of lines and circles.

Analytic Geometry generalizes coordinate methods to higher dimensions with coordinate systems empowering geometric visualization and problem-solving across mathematics, science, and technology. Let us now delve into trigonometry and its deep connections with geometric concepts.

Transformational Geometry

Examining the changes wrought by geometric transformations like translations, rotations, reflections, and dilations yields deep insights. Some key facts:

Translations slide points along a constant direction vector without changing distances, angles, or orientation. Combined translations generate euclidean motions.

Rotations pivot around a fixed point, leaving angles unchanged but "spinning" positions. The rotation amount r is measured anticlockwise in radians or degrees. Full rotations equal 2π radians or 360 degrees.

Reflections flip points across a line called the mirror, leaving distances unchanged while reversing the sense of angles. Glide reflections compose a reflection and translation.

Dilations or "scaling" uniformly resize objects proportionally about a fixed center point. The scale factor s describes how many times lengths inflate/deflate.

Isometries encompass rigid motions, keeping shapes congruent through translations, rotations, and reflections. Similarities allow scaling, too, while maintaining proportional angles.

Understanding properties preserved versus changed distinguishes these map types. Their operations compose new transformations useful for crystallography, kinematics, and computer graphics. Representing geometric objects unchanged under rigid motions sparks ideas on groups, vectors, and symmetries.

Analytic Geometry

While geometry describes spatial qualities visually, analytic methods represent points and their transformations using algebraic tools like coordinates and equations. This marries two ancient topics into a unified framework with far-reaching implications. Some highlights:

Cartesian Coordinates locate points in two dimensions using ordered pairs (x, y). Three or higher dimensions generalize this numeric indexing.

Equations of Lines emerge by plugging cartesian coordinates into linear relationships between x and y. Slopes, perpendicular bisectors, and intersections define these polynomial forms.

Conic Sections model ellipses, parabolas, and hyperbolas through quadric equations, obtaining shapes from planar slices through a circular double-napped cone. Projects like spaceflight rely on their elliptical orbits.

Space Curves trace ribbons or trajectories through 3D worlds defined parametrically or using cylindrical/spherical coordinates. These describe particle motions and surfaces from screws to Mobius bands to Möbius strips.

Matrices and Vectors provide a compact notation for analyzing groups of transformations like rotations, projections, and affinities performed simultaneously on geometries. Linear algebra fundamentally changed geometry's character.

Analytic techniques enable the formulation of geometric reasoning, symbolically leading to far-reaching generalizations and applications in many domains today. Together, geometry and analysis comprise the foundation for technical graphics, computer imaging, and deep mathematical structures across fields.

Non-Euclidean Geometry

While classical geometry operated on Euclid's postulates like the parallel line property, modern mathematics has expanded the scope through alternate geometries challenging those assumptions. Two major examples:

Elliptic Geometry arises on surfaces like spheres where through a point of a line, pass no parallels. Inside triangles, angles sum greater than 180 degrees growing with curvature. These find use in general relativity.

Hyperbolic Geometry occupies negative curvature spaces like pseudospheres or Poincaré disks where parallels diverge. Hyperbolic trigonometry applies to fractals, networks, and tilings containing exponentially more objects at finer scales.

More broadly, Riemannian Geometry handles all types of curved spaces, unifying Euclidean, spherical, and hyperbolic cases through intrinsic metrics and covariant derivatives. It describes gravitation, cosmology, manifolds and geometric flows with implications across branches today. Stepping outside familiar axioms sparked novel insights.

Trigonometry

Etymologically coming from Greek words for "triangle" and "measurement," trigonometry studies relationships between side lengths and angles in triangles, particularly right triangles containing one 90° angle. The main terms are:

Trigonometric Functions:

Trigonometry focuses on the relationship between angles and sides within triangles, particularly right triangles. The three primary trigonometric ratios, along with their inverses, form the foundation of this field:

- **Sine (sin):** This ratio is defined as the opposite side (side facing the right angle) divided by the hypotenuse (longest side) of a right triangle. In the notation we introduced earlier, sin(angle) = a / c.
- **Cosine (cos):** This ratio is defined as the adjacent side (side next to the right angle) divided by the hypotenuse of a right triangle. Continuing with our notation, cos(angle) = b / c.
- **Tangent (tan):** This ratio is defined as the opposite side divided by the adjacent side of a right triangle. Therefore, tan(angle) = a / b.

These ratios hold true for all right triangles with the same corresponding angles, regardless of the actual side lengths. In other words, if you have a right triangle and know the measure of one angle, you can use these ratios to calculate the lengths of the other sides relative to each other. There are also inverse trigonometric functions (arcsin, arccos, arctan) that can be used to find the angle measure given the ratio of two sides.

- Reference Angles: Any angle θ can be related to its reference angle in the standard position by reflecting over the x-axis, thus staying within the range $0 \leq \theta \leq 90°$.
- Unit Circle: Graphing trig functions with θ as the central angle yields the unit circle where ratios vary as x-y coordinates on the circumference of a circle with radius 1 centered at the origin. This connects trigonometry and complex numbers.
- Special Identities: Relationships like $\sin 2\theta + \cos 2\theta = 1$ arise from properties of right triangles inscribed in the unit circle. Other Pythagorean identities simplify expressions through cancellation.
- Periodicity: Trig functions repeat values over an angular period of 360° or 2π radians, with frequencies halving at 180° or π. This periodic nature underpins waves.

- Inverse Functions: Relations involving arcsine, arccosine, and arctangent undo the trig functions to find the angle θ given only its ratio output, with restricted domains due to periodicity.
- Trigonometric Form: Using trig identities, expressions can be manipulated into forms like sum and difference of angles, half-angle, and double-angle, opening new problem-solving options.

Geometry and trigonometry intersect through such notions as the 30-60-90 right triangle arising from dividing an equilateral triangle into six 30° sectors, yielding ratio relationships like √3 for the tangent. The law of sines and cosines extends these ratios to any triangle, not just right triangles. Polar coordinates also fuse trig and geometry via angle-radius representation of points.

Applications of Geometry and Trigonometry

The precision, rigor and abstraction foundational to mathematics also prove intensely practical. Geometry and trigonometry undergird diverse applications spanning science, technology, art, and more. A sampling:

- Architecture – From building blueprints to vaulted structures, architects leverage geometric properties for aesthetic design and engineering feasibility. Building techniques from different cultures around the world utilize geometry in diverse and innovative ways.
- Cartography – Map projections transform global spheres into planar representations navigated using coordinate geometry and trigonometric computations. Different map projections prioritize accuracy for specific geometric properties like angles, areas, or distances depending on the intended use of the map.
- Engineering – Leveraging properties like static equilibrium, projectile motion simulation, and spatial reasoning across mechanical, electrical, and civil design domains. Engineers apply geometry and trigonometry to solve problems involving force, motion, stress analysis, and more through analytical modeling and computer-aided design tools.
- Astronomy – Orbital mechanic systems, celestial navigation, and telescope modeling rely on the geometry of conic sections and spherical trigonometric formations. Astronomers also use geometry to analyze data from space probes and calculate trajectories for interplanetary travel.

- Computer Graphics – Rendering, gaming, and virtual/augmented reality all immerse users in utilizing underlying principles from projective, Euclidean, and non-Euclidean geometries. Advanced techniques like ray tracing and curvature flows apply geometry at microscales for photorealistic simulations.
- Art – Sculptures, paintings, textures, and patterns decorate our world, invoking symmetry groups, fractals, and tilings arising from geometry's transformations and behaviors. Artists through the ages have been inspired by geometric forms found in nature and architecture.

PART IV
GO
Take the Digital SAT

PRACTICE TEST

Section 1: Reading and Writing Test – Module 1

32 Minutes, 27 Questions

Directions

The questions in this section address a number of important reading and writing skills. Each question includes one or more passages, which may include a table or graph. Read each passage and question carefully, and then choose the best answer to the question based on the passage(s). All questions in this section are multiple-choice with four answer choices. Each question has a single best answer.

QUESTION 1

Recently, researchers analyzed data collected by the European Space Agency's ExoMars rover to understand seismic activity on Venus, known as venusquakes. The findings revealed that the venusquakes all originated from a single region on the planet. This discovery was unexpected for researchers, who had anticipated that the venusquakes would occur in various locations due to the planet's cooling surface. Now, scientists theorize that there might be active magma flows deep beneath Venus's surface causing the venusquakes.

According to the text, what was surprising to researchers studying the seismic activity data from the European Space Agency's ExoMars rover?

A) The surface temperature of Venus has been increasing.

B) There were various types of seismic waves causing venusquakes.

C) The ExoMars rover collected less data than researchers had anticipated.

D) All the venusquakes originated from the same region on the planet.

QUESTION 2

The ancient writing system used in the Indus Valley civilization in modern-day Pakistan and northwest India had a symbol for the number zero. The earliest known instance of the symbol dates back over 2,500 years. At that time, almost none of the writing systems elsewhere in the world had a zero symbol. Some historians propose that Indus Valley mathematicians might have inherited it from the Mesopotamian civilization, which thrived in the region 3,000–4,000 years ago.

According to the text, what do some historians suggest about the Indus Valley civilization?

A) The Indus Valley civilization acquired the use of zero from the Mesopotamian civilization.

B) The Indus Valley civilization valued its historians more than its mathematicians.

C) The Indus Valley civilization was highly secretive about its intellectual achievements.

D) The Indus Valley civilization attempted to introduce its writing system to other civilizations.

QUESTION 3

"The Bet" is an 1889 short story by Anton Chekhov. In the story, a merchant is described as being very upset about something: _____

Which quotation from "The Bet" most effectively illustrates the claim?

A) "Then the merchant cautiously broke the seals off the door and put the key in the keyhole."

B) "It struck three o'clock, the merchant listened; everyone was asleep in the house and nothing could be heard outside but the rustling of the chilled trees."

C) "The merchant, spoilt and frivolous, with millions beyond his reckoning, was delighted at the bet."

D) "When [the merchant] got home he lay on his bed, but his tears and emotion kept him for hours from sleeping."

QUESTION 4

Partial List of Candidate Species for De-extinction

Common name	Scientific name	Became extinct
Dodo	Raphus cucullatus	1681
Baiji	Lipotes vexillifer	2006
Tasmanian tiger	Thylacinus cynocephalus	1936
Woolly rhinoceros	Coelodonta antiquitatis	10,000 years before present
Giant ground sloth	Megatherium americanum	8,000 years before present

The passage of time is among the many challenges faced by scientists working on de-extinction efforts—that is, attempts to use breeding or a mix of cloning and genetic engineering to bring back extinct species. Specifically, researchers worry that the longer a species has been extinct, the less likely a suitable habitat still exists for that species. Among candidate species for de-extinction, this problem would be especially concerning for the _____

Which choice most effectively uses data from the table to complete the statement?

A) Tasmanian tiger (Thylacinus cynocephalus), which became extinct only a few years before the Baiji (Lipotes vexillifer).

B) Woolly rhinoceros (Coelodonta antiquitatis), which became extinct 10,000 years ago.

C) Giant ground sloth (Megatherium americanum), which became extinct several thousand years before the woolly rhinoceros (Coelodonta antiquitatis).

D) Dodo (Raphus cucullatus), which became extinct in 1681.

QUESTION 5

"The Yellow Wallpaper" is an 1892 short story by Charlotte Perkins Gilman. In the story, the narrator expresses mixed feelings about her surroundings: _____

Which quotation from "The Yellow Wallpaper" most effectively illustrates the claim?

A) "This wallpaper has a kind of sub-pattern in a different shade, a particularly irritating one, for you can only see it in certain lights, and not clearly then."
B) "By moonlight—the moon shines in all night when there is a moon—I wouldn't know it was the same paper."
C) "I'm really getting quite fond of the big room, all but that horrid [wall]paper."
D) "The color is repellant, almost revolting; a smouldering, unclean yellow, strangely faded by the slow-turning sunlight."

QUESTION 6

The Huronian glaciation was a period of extreme cooling approximately 2.4 to 2.1 billion years ago on Earth. Some scientists argue that a massive volcanic eruption triggered the cooling. Others disagree, partly because there is no conclusive evidence of such an eruption dating to the onset of the period. In 2019, a team led by Dr. Elena Martinez discovered a 25-mile-wide caldera beneath the Pacific Ocean. The scientists who believe a volcanic eruption caused the Huronian glaciation claim that this discovery supports their view. However, Martinez's team hasn't yet been able to determine the age of the caldera. Therefore, the team suggests that _____

Which choice most logically completes the text?

A) it can't be concluded that the eruption that formed the caldera was connected to the onset of the Huronian glaciation.
B) it can't be determined whether a volcanic eruption could create a caldera as large as 25 miles wide.
C) scientists have ignored the possibility that something other than a volcanic eruption could have formed the caldera.
D) the scientists who believe a volcanic eruption caused the Huronian glaciation have made incorrect assumptions about when the period began.

QUESTION 7

In 2018, evolutionary biologist Dr. James Lee and his team investigated the development of the spleen, an organ involved in the immune system, in various mammalian species. Studying 412 species, the team found that the spleen has appeared independently across multiple lineages in separate instances and, significantly, hasn't disappeared after emerging in specific lineages. Moreover, the team determined that species with the organ tend to have higher concentrations of lymphoid tissue, which supports immune responses, in the spleen. Therefore, the team hypothesized that the spleen likely _____

Which choice most logically completes the text?

A) was once present in many nonmammal species but has since disappeared from those lineages.

B) has been preserved in certain mammal species because it benefits their immune systems.

C) will emerge in a greater number of mammal species because it may serve a necessary function in the immune system.

D) produced higher concentrations of lymphoid tissue in mammals in the past than it does currently.

QUESTION 8

Some ethicists hold that the moral goodness of an individual's actions depends solely on whether the actions themselves are good, irrespective of the context in which they are carried out. Philosopher Dr. Angela Ramirez has shown that surviving works of Inca (Quechua) philosophy express a very different view. Ramirez reveals that these works posit an ethical system in which an individual's actions are judged in light of how well they accord with the individual's role in society and how well they contribute to the community. To the extent that these works are representative of Inca thought, Ramirez's analysis suggests that _____

Which choice most logically completes the text?

A) the Incas would have disputed the idea that the morality of an individual's actions can be assessed by appealing to standards of behavior that are independent of the individual's social circumstances.

B) the Incas would not have accepted the notion that the morality of an individual's actions can be fairly evaluated by people who do not live in the same society as that individual.

C) actions by members of Inca society who contributed a great deal to their community could be judged as morally good even if those actions were inconsistent with behaviors the Incas regarded as good in all contexts.

D) similar actions performed by people in different social roles in Inca society would have been regarded as morally equivalent unless those actions led to different outcomes for the community.

QUESTION 9

In 2017, Dr. Tran Nguyen became the fifteenth secretary-general of the Association of Southeast Asian Nations (ASEAN), making _____ the first time the organization would appoint a Vietnamese leader.

Which choice completes the text so that it conforms to the conventions of Standard English?

A) these
B) those
C) this
D) some

QUESTION 10

In 1939, physicist Dr. Maria Hernandez invented a superconducting material that was featured in a number of applications, from medical imaging to quantum computing. A decade later, Hernandez _____ her technology to develop the world's first quantum computer.

Which choice completes the text so that it conforms to the conventions of Standard English?

A) used
B) to have used
C) to use
D) using

QUESTION 11

An online content creator who uses copyrighted images without permission risks being demonetized (prohibited from including paid advertisements in content). The best way to avoid demonetization is to choose images from the public domain. Using one of these noncopyrighted images _____ a creator won't lose advertising revenue.

Which choice completes the text so that it conforms to the conventions of Standard English?

A) are ensuring
B) have ensured
C) ensure
D) ensures

QUESTION 12

In the music video for the song "Cultural Pulse" by Alex Rivera, the singer lists 150 political and cultural references. Such iconic references, cited in rapid and frenetic procession by the musician, who is seated thoughtfully at a park bench, _____ key moments and personalities of the twenty-first century.

Which choice completes the text so that it conforms to the conventions of Standard English?

A) represents
B) has represented
C) was representing
D) represent

QUESTION 13

What makes the theremin a unique musical instrument? You play it without touching it. When you place your _____ the pitch will shift as your hands move through the air.

Which choice completes the text with the most logical transition?

A) hand's between the two antenna's,
B) hands between the two antennas,
C) hands' between the two antennas',
D) hands' between the two antennas,

QUESTION 14

Long attributed to Élisabeth Vigée Le Brun, the preeminent portrait painter of her day, the 1789 painting "Portrait of a Young Woman" gained fresh attention in the 2000s when art historians discovered that the painting—which depicts a solitary young woman reading—was actually the work of little-known French portrait _____ Marie-Guillemine Benoist (1768–1826).

Which choice completes the text so that it conforms to the conventions of Standard English?

A) artist—
B) artist
C) artist:
D) artist,

QUESTION 15

In 1990, conceptual artist Lee Mingwei asked thirty individuals, all of whom had never seen a rainbow, to describe "their image of a rainbow" in vivid detail. Lee paired excerpts of these conversations with photographs—both of interviewees and the items they _____ to powerful effect in his exhibition "Rainbows in the Dark."

Which choice completes the text so that it conforms to the conventions of Standard English?

A) described, from flowers to rain to light
B) described, from flowers to rain to light—
C) described—from flowers to rain to light,
D) described: from flowers to rain to light

QUESTION 16

Historians agree that the playwright William Shakespeare was exaggerating when he claimed to have invented the English sonnet. No one can deny, _____ that Shakespeare's innovative plays and remarkable use of language helped shape English literature as a genre during its early years.

Which choice completes the text with the most logical transition?

A) therefore,
B) in the second place,
C) in other words,
D) though,

QUESTION 17

Celebrated Pueblo potter Maria Martinez (1887–1980) made her signature black-on-black ceramic vessels using a firing technique called reduction firing. This technique involves smothering the flame surrounding the clay vessel. _____ the vessel takes on a shiny, black hue.

Which choice completes the text with the most logical transition?

A) On the contrary,
B) For example,
C) Previously,
D) As a result,

QUESTION 18

According to Duverger's law, countries with single-ballot majoritarian elections for single-member districts tend to polarize into two-party systems, wherein dueling political parties consistently dominate the political system. _____ countries with proportional-representation electoral systems tend to support multi-partyism, under which power gets distributed among many political parties.

Which choice completes the text with the most logical transition?

A) Subsequently,
B) Conversely,
C) For instance,
D) In other words,

QUESTION 19

A turtle shell appears external to the animal, protecting its body like armor. _____ the shell is often incorrectly assumed to be an exoskeleton, a rigid outer casing like that of a crustacean or an insect, when in fact it is an endoskeleton, a part of the turtle's internal bone structure, more akin to a spine or a pair of ribs.

Which choice completes the text with the most logical transition?

A) That being said,
B) However,
C) For instance,
D) Hence,

QUESTION 20

Carnivorous theropod dinosaurs could grow more than 40 feet long and weigh up to 10 tons, and some researchers have attributed the evolution of theropods to such massive sizes to increased prey availability resulting from high levels of atmospheric oxygen during the

Cretaceous period. However, there is no evidence of significant spikes in oxygen levels coinciding with relevant periods in theropod evolution, such as when the first large theropods appeared, when several theropod lineages underwent further evolution toward gigantism, or when theropods reached their maximum known sizes, suggesting that _____

Which choice most logically completes the text?

A) fluctuations in atmospheric oxygen affected different theropod lineages differently.

B) the evolution of larger body sizes in theropods did not depend on increased atmospheric oxygen.

C) atmospheric oxygen was higher when the largest known theropods lived than it was when the first theropods appeared.

D) theropods probably would not have evolved to such immense sizes if atmospheric oxygen had been even slightly higher.

QUESTION 21

In documents called judicial decisions, judges explain the reasoning behind their legal rulings, and in those explanations, they sometimes cite and discuss historical and contemporary philosophers. Legal scholar and philosopher Dr. Michael Johnson argues that while judges are naturally inclined to mention philosophers whose views align with their own positions, the strongest judicial decisions consider and rebut potential objections; discussing philosophers whose views conflict with judges' views could therefore _____

Which choice most logically completes the text?

A) allow judges to craft judicial decisions without needing to consult philosophical works.

B) help judges improve the arguments they put forward in their judicial decisions.

C) make judicial decisions more comprehensible to readers without legal or philosophical training.

D) bring judicial decisions in line with views that are broadly held among philosophers.

QUESTION 22

Public-awareness campaigns about the need to reduce single-use plastics can be successful, says researcher Emily White of Stanford University in the United States, when these campaigns give consumers a choice: for example, Germany achieved a 50 percent reduction in plastic-bag use after cashiers were instructed to ask customers whether _____ wanted a bag.

Which choice completes the text so that it conforms to the conventions of Standard English?

A) they
B) one
C) you
D) it

QUESTION 23

In ancient Rome, a Stoic was a follower of Zeno, a philosopher whose beliefs revolved around the pursuit of virtue. Zeno defined virtue as "the absence of passion in the mind and of trouble in the _____ that all life's virtues derived from this absence.

Which choice completes the text so that it conforms to the conventions of Standard English?

A) soul," positing
B) soul": positing
C) soul"; positing
D) soul." Positing

QUESTION 24

(1) The company launched a new product. (2) They conducted market research beforehand. (3) Sales exceeded expectations.

Which is the correct order of sentences to make the passage logical?

A) 1, 2, 3
B) 2, 1, 3
C) 3, 1, 2
D) 2, 3, 1

QUESTION 25

Choose the sentence that uses formal language.

She was super tired after the long day.

B) She was extremely fatigued after the lengthy day.
C) She was really tired after the long day.
D) She was kinda tired after the long day.

QUESTION 26

Select the sentence that avoids redundancy.

A) He made a brief summary of the main points.

B) He summarized the main points.

C) He gave a brief and short summary of the main points.

D) He made a short summary of the main points.

QUESTION 27

Choose the word that best completes the sentence.

The lawyer's argument was ___, leaving no room for doubt about her client's innocence.

A) ambiguous

B) conclusive

C) confusing

D) weak

Section 1: Reading and Writing Test – Module 2

32 Minutes, 27 Questions

Directions

The questions in this section address a number of important reading and writing skills. Each question includes one or more passages, which may include a table or graph. Read each passage and question carefully, and then choose the best answer to the question based on the passage(s). All questions in this section are multiple-choice with four answer choices. Each question has a single best answer.

QUESTION 1

In the early 20th century, the concept of urban planning emerged as a response to the rapid industrialization and urbanization that characterized the period. Urban planners sought to design cities that would be more efficient, healthier, and aesthetically pleasing. One of the leading figures in this movement was Ebenezer Howard, whose vision of the "garden city" combined the best elements of town and country living.

What was the primary goal of urban planners in the early 20th century?

    A) To reduce the population of cities
    B) To create more rural areas
    C) To design cities that are more efficient and healthy
    D) To demolish existing urban structures

QUESTION 2

The artist's work was characterized by its use of vibrant colors and **intricate** patterns.

In the passage, the word "intricate" most nearly means:

    A) simple
    B) complex
    C) dull
    D) random

QUESTION 3

The introduction of the assembly line by Henry Ford revolutionized the automobile industry, making cars affordable for the average American and significantly increasing production rates.

What is the main idea of the passage?

A) Henry Ford invented the car.

B) The assembly line made cars cheaper and increased production.

C) Car production was slow before the assembly line.

D) Henry Ford's cars were very expensive.

QUESTION 4

Despite the significant advances in renewable energy technology, many countries still rely heavily on fossil fuels for their energy needs. This reliance poses a challenge to efforts aimed at reducing carbon emissions and combating climate change.

It can be inferred from the passage that:

A) Renewable energy is the primary source of energy worldwide.

B) Fossil fuels are no longer used in most countries.

C) Reducing carbon emissions is difficult due to the reliance on fossil fuels.

D) Renewable energy technology has not advanced significantly.

QUESTION 5

The author's detailed description of the rainforests' biodiversity aims to highlight the importance of conservation efforts.

The author's primary purpose in the passage is to:

A) entertain with stories of rainforests

B) persuade readers to support conservation

C) inform about the history of rainforests

D) criticize government policies

QUESTION 6

Studies have shown that students who participate in extracurricular activities tend to have higher academic performance than those who do not.

Which piece of evidence would best support this claim?

    A) A survey of student interests
    B) Data showing academic performance of students involved in extracurricular activities
    C) Anecdotal stories of successful students
    D) Historical trends in education

QUESTION 7

The first section of the article discusses the causes of climate change, while the second section focuses on potential solutions.

    A) By comparing and contrasting two viewpoints
    B) By presenting a problem and then a solution
    C) By listing a series of events in chronological order
    D) By describing a process in step-by-step detail

QUESTION 8

The author's tone in the passage is one of cautious optimism, acknowledging the challenges ahead but expressing hope for future progress.

The tone of the passage can best be described as:

    A) indifferent
    B) pessimistic
    C) cautiously optimistic
    D) critical

QUESTION 9

The novel explores themes of identity and self-discovery as the protagonist embarks on a journey to uncover their true self.

The main theme of the novel is:

    A) adventure
    B) identity and self-discovery
    C) friendship
    D) survival

QUESTION 10

Passage 1:
The first text argues that technology has greatly improved communication, making it easier for people to stay connected.

Passage 2:
The second text claims that technology has created barriers to genuine human interaction, leading to isolation.

How do the two texts differ in their views on technology's impact on communication?

    A) The first text sees it as positive, while the second sees it as negative.
    B) Both texts view it positively.
    C) Both texts view it negatively.
    D) The first text sees it as negative, while the second sees it as positive.

QUESTION 11

Select the sentence with the correct use of the semicolon.

    A) She loves reading; she finds it relaxing.
    B) She loves reading, she finds it relaxing.
    C) She loves reading; and she finds it relaxing.
    D) She loves reading she finds it relaxing.

QUESTION 12

Which sentence is punctuated correctly?

    A) My favorite colors are blue, green and red.

    B) My favorite colors are blue; green, and red.

    C) My favorite colors are; blue, green, and red.

    D) My favorite colors are blue, green, and red.

QUESTION 13

Identify the sentence that is a fragment.

    A) Running through the park, she felt free and happy.

    B) Although he was tired after a long day at work.

    C) She enjoys painting in her free time.

    D) The dog barked loudly all night.

QUESTION 14

Choose the sentence that maintains parallel structure.

    A) She likes reading, to jog, and cooking.

    B) She likes reading, jogging, and cooking.

    C) She likes to read, jog, and cooking.

    D) She likes to read, jogging, and to cook.

QUESTION 15

Select the sentence with the correct verb tense.

    A) By the time he arrived, the train leaves.

    B) By the time he arrived, the train had left.

    C) By the time he arrived, the train will leave.

    D) By the time he arrived, the train leaves.

QUESTION 16

Identify the sentence with correct subject–verb agreement.

    A) The group of students are going on a trip.

    B) The group of students is going on a trip.

    C) The group of students were going on a trip.

    D) The group of students have going on a trip.

QUESTION 17

Choose the sentence with correct pronoun agreement.

    A) Each student must bring their own lunch.

    B) Each student must bring his or her own lunch.

    C) Each student must bring their own lunches.

    D) Each student must bring his and her own lunch.

QUESTION 18

Select the sentence with the correct placement of the modifier.

    A) She almost drove her kids to school every day.

    B) She drove her kids to school almost every day.

    C) She drove almost her kids to school every day.

    D) She drove her kids almost to school every day.

QUESTION 19

Choose the most effective sentence.

    A) Because she was late, she missed the bus, and she had to walk to school.

    B) She missed the bus and had to walk to school because she was late.

    C) She was late, she missed the bus, and she had to walk to school.

    D) Late she was, missed the bus, and had to walk to school.

QUESTION 20

Select the most concise sentence.

    A) Due to the fact that it was raining, we decided to stay indoors.

    B) Because it was raining, we decided to stay indoors.

    C) Due to the fact that it was raining, we made the decision to stay indoors.

    D) Because it was raining, we made the decision to stay indoors.

QUESTION 21

Which is the best way to combine the following sentences?

"She enjoys hiking. She also enjoys swimming."

    A) She enjoys hiking, and enjoys swimming.

    B) She enjoys hiking and also enjoys swimming.

    C) She enjoys both hiking and swimming.

    D) She enjoys hiking; she also enjoys swimming.

QUESTION 22

The scientist conducted numerous experiments. **Nevertheless**, the results were inconclusive.

Which transition word would best replace "Nevertheless" to indicate a contrast?

    A) Furthermore

    B) However

    C) In addition

    D) Therefore

QUESTION 23

The politician's rhetoric was powerful, but many doubted his sincerity.

In the passage, the word "rhetoric" most nearly means:

    A) speaking

    B) honesty

    C) silence

    D) insincerity

QUESTION 24

American scientists Robert Wilson and Arno Penzias won the Nobel Prize in part for their 1965 discovery of the cosmic microwave background radiation, but it is misleading to say that Wilson and Penzias discovered the radiation. _____ findings were based on earlier theoretical predictions made by other physicists.

Which choice completes the text so that it conforms to the conventions of Standard English?

A) They're
B) It's
C) Their
D) Its

QUESTION 25

In 1951, African American actress Dorothy Dandridge, who had portrayed numerous supporting characters but never a leading role, finally got a starring role in Twentieth Century-Fox's Bright Road, a film that _____ "expanded the range of possibilities for African American images on screen."

Which choice completes the text so that it conforms to the conventions of Standard English?

A) critic, John Doe, claims
B) critic, John Doe, claims,
C) critic John Doe claims
D) critic John Doe, claims,

QUESTION 26

In 1720, the price of South Sea Company shares skyrocketed in London, with single shares selling for up to the equivalent of $1 million in today's US dollars. Some historians _____ that this "South Sea Bubble" was the first historical instance of an asset bubble, which occurs when investors drive prices to highs not supported by actual demand.

Which choice completes the text so that it conforms to the conventions of Standard English?

A) claiming
B) claim
C) having claimed
D) to claim

QUESTION 27

Researchers studying magnetosensation have determined why some soil-dwelling nematodes in the Northern Hemisphere move in the opposite direction of Earth's magnetic field when searching for _____ in the Southern Hemisphere, the magnetic field points down, into the ground, but in the Northern Hemisphere, it points up, toward the surface and away from nematodes' food sources.

Which choice completes the text so that it conforms to the conventions of Standard English?

    A) food:

    B) food,

    C) food while

    D) food

Section 2: Math Test- Module 1

35 Minutes, 22 Questions

Direction

For questions 1 through 15, do each task, select the best response from the list of options, and mark the matching bubble on your answer sheet. Solve the problems in questions 16 through 20 and record your solution in the grid on the answer sheet. Kindly consult the instructions on how to submit your responses in the grid before question 16. You can do scratch work in any available place in your test booklet.

Notes

Unless otherwise indicated:

- All variables and expressions represent real numbers.
- Figures provided are drawn to scale.
- All figures lie in a plane.
- The domain of a given function f is the set of all real numbers x for which is a real number.

Reference

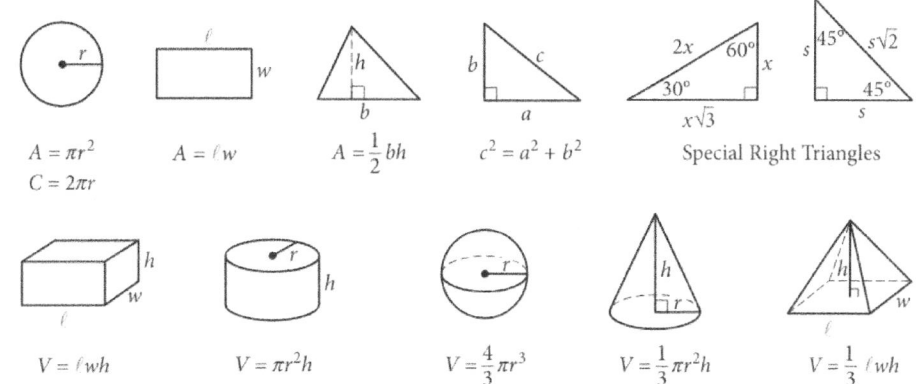

360 degrees is the number of arc degrees in a circle.

A circle has two radians of arc, or 2p.

A triangle's total angle measurements, expressed in degrees, equals 180.

For multiple-choice questions, solve each problem, select the correct answer from the options provided, and then circle your answer in this book. Only circle one answer per question. If you change your mind, completely erase the previous circle. You will not receive credit for questions with more than one answer circled or for questions with no answer circled.

For student-produced response questions, solve each problem and write your answer next to or under the question in the test book as follows:

- Do not include symbols such as a percent sign, comma, or dollar sign in your circled answer.
- Once you've written your answer, circle it clearly. You will not receive credit for anything written outside the circle or for any questions with more than one circled answer.
- If you find more than one correct answer, write and circle only one.
- Your answer can be up to 5 characters for a positive answer and up to 6 characters (including the negative sign) for a negative answer.
- If your answer is a fraction that exceeds the character limit (over 5 characters for positive, 6 characters for negative), write the decimal equivalent.
- If your answer is a decimal that exceeds the character limit (over 5 characters for positive, 6 characters for negative), truncate or round it to the fourth digit.
- If your answer is a mixed number (such as 3½), write it as an improper fraction (7/2) or its decimal equivalent (3.5).

1. $2z + 1 = z$

For what value of z does the above equation hold true?

(A) –2
B) –1
C) 1/2
D) 1/2

2. We want to buy a $300 television, and we want to pay a $60 down payment and $30 every week after that. Finding the amount of weekly payments, w, necessary to finish the transaction, assuming no taxes or fees, can be done using which of the following equations?

A) $300 = 30w - 60$
B) $300 = 30w$
C) $300 = 30 + 60w$
D) $300 = 60 - 30$

3.

Shipping Charges

Merchandise weight (pounds)	Shipping charge
5	$16.94
10	$21.89
20	$31.79
40	$51.59

An online merchant selling sporting products has shipping costs displayed in the table above. In terms of relationships, the shipping charge and the weight of the goods. With an order weighing x pounds in items, what function may be used to calculate the total delivery price f(x), expressed in dollars?

    A) f(x) = 0.99x
    B) f(x) = 0.99x + 11.99
    C) f(x) = 3.39
    D) f(x) = 3.39 + 16.94

4.

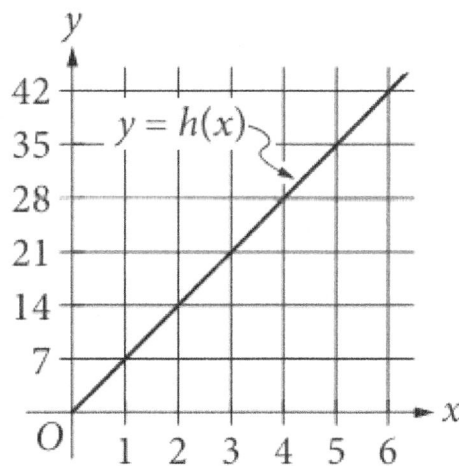

The relationship for cylindrical Doric columns between the height h =(x), in feet, and the base diameter x, in feet, is represented by the line in the xy-plane above. Greek classical architecture features columns. The height of a Doric column with a base diameter of five feet is how much higher than the height of a Doric column with a base diameter of two feet?

    A) 7 feet
    B) 14 feet
    C) 21 feet
    D) Two dozen feet

5. $\sqrt{9x^2}$.

For each given x > 0, which of the following expressions is equivalent?

    A) 3x

    B) 3x2

    C) 18x

    D) 18x4

6. $\frac{x^2-1}{x-1}$ which of the following values of x results in an undefined expression or simplifies uniquely??

    A) –3

    B) 0

    C) 1

    D) –3 and –1

7.

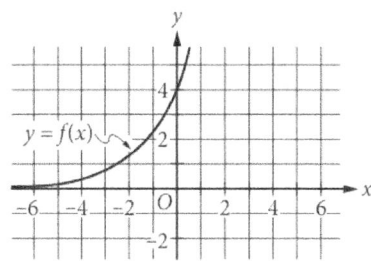

The graph of y = f (x) is shown in the xy-plane. What is the value of f(0)?

    A) 0

    B) 2

    C) 3

    D) 4

8.

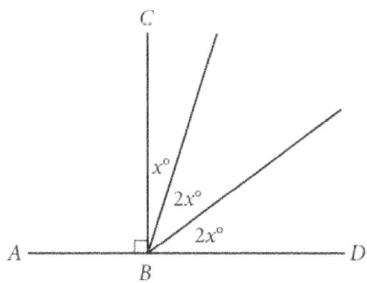

Point B on AD in the above figure. How much is 3x worth?

   A) 18
   B) 36
   D) 54
   D) 72

9.

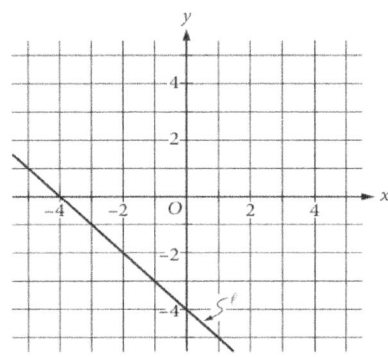

Which of the following describes the equation of a line in the above xy plane?

   A) x − y = −4
   B) x − y = 4
   C) x + y = −4
   D) x + y = 4

10.

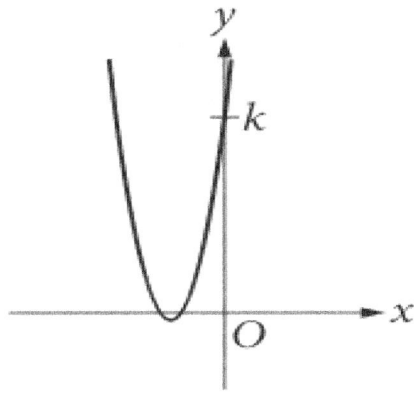

The $y = 2x^2 + 10x + 12$ graph is displayed. What is the value of k if the graph crosses the y-axis at the point (0, k)?

   A) 2
   B) 6
   C) 10
   D) 12

11. A circle with radius 2 and center (5, 7) is in the xy plane. Which of the following is a circle equation?

   A) $(x-5)^2 + (x-7)^2 = 4$
   B) $(x+5)^2 + (x+7)^2 = 4$
   C) $(x-5)^2 + (x-7)^2 = 2$
   D) $(x+5)^2 + (x+7)^2 = 2$

12.

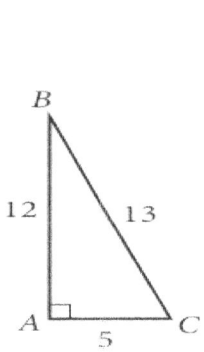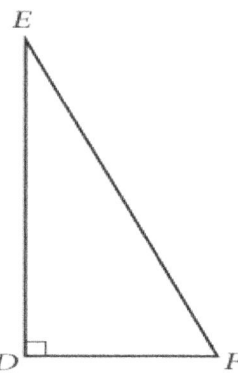

Triangle DEF and triangle ABC in the preceding illustration are comparable. How much is cos(E) worth?

   A) 12/5
   B) 5/12
   C) 5/12
   D) 5/13

13. The function f (x) = x2 + 5x + 4 has two x-intercepts on its graph in the xy-plane. What is the

X-intercepts' distance from one another?

   A), 1
   B), 2
   C), 3
   D) 4

14. $\sqrt{4x} = x - 3$

Which values of x satisfy the given equation in all cases?

I. 1

II. 9

   A) I only,

   B) II only,

   C) I and II,

   D) Neither I nor II

15. $-3x+y=6$, $ax+2y=4$

A is a constant in the given set of equations. Which of the following values does the system not have a solution for?

   A) −6,

   B) −3,

   C) −3,

   D) −6

16. $T = 5c + 12f$

A producer sent pieces of a specific product to Two places. The formula above displays the total cost of shipping, expressed in dollars, for sending c units to the location that is closer and f units to the site that is farther away. How many units were transported to the closer location if 3000 units were shipped to the distant location and the total shipping cost was $47,000?

17. $|2x+1| = 5$.

What is the value of $|a - b|$ if a and b are the solutions to the preceding equation?

18. Juan paid $200 for an antique that was worth that much at the time. Annually, the worth of the value of an antique is predicted to rise by 10% from the previous year. Given an antique and two years after purchase, its anticipated worth in dollars is given by the equation 200a, where an is a constant. What does an a have worth?

19. 2x+3y=1200,

3x+2y=1300

What is the value of 5x y + 5 based on the preceding system of equations?

20. What is the value of (u–t) $(u^2 - t^2)$ if u +t = 5 and u – t = 2?

21.

x	a	$3a$	$5a$
y	0	$-a$	$-2a$

In the table above, where an is a constant, several values of x and their matching values of y are displayed. Should x and y have a linear connection? Which equation in the list below best captures the relationship?

A) x+2y=a

B) x + 2y = 5a

C) 2x - y = -5a

D) 2x - y =7a

22.

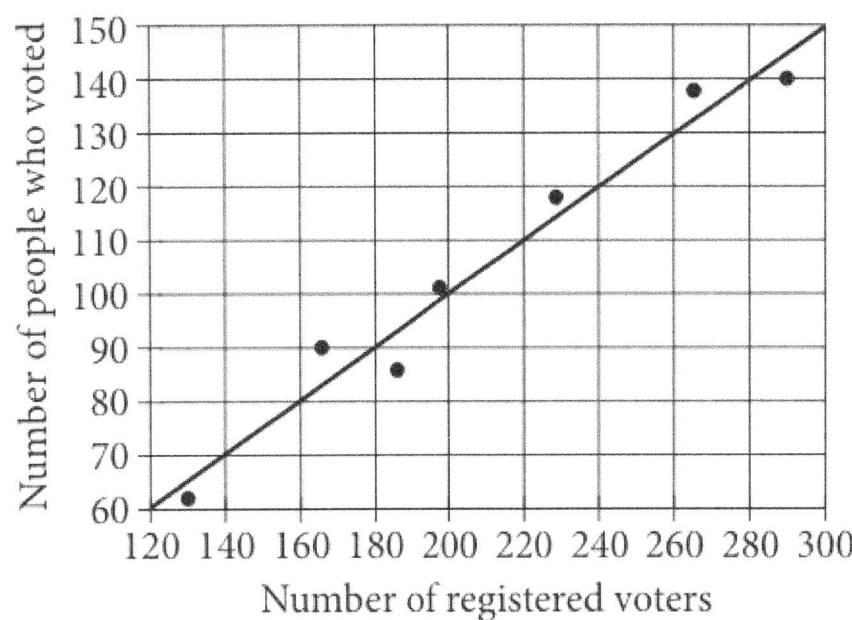

In the accompanying scatterplot, seven districts within a town are represented by the numbers of registered voters (x) and those who cast ballots in the most recent election (y). One line of the data's best fit is also displayed. Of the following, which one might be the line of the best-fit equation?

A) $y = -0.5x$

B) $y = 0.5x$

C) $y = -2.5x$

D) $y = 2x$

Section 2: Math Test- Module 1

35 Minutes, 22 Questions

Direction

For questions 1 through 15, do each task, select the best response from the list of options, and mark the matching bubble on your answer sheet. Solve the problems in questions 16 through 20 and record your solution in the grid on the answer sheet. Kindly consult the instructions on how to submit your responses in the grid before question 16. You can do scratch work in any available place in your test booklet.

Notes

Unless otherwise indicated:

- All variables and expressions represent real numbers.
- Figures provided are drawn to scale.
- All figures lie in a plane.
- The domain of a given function f is the set of all real numbers x for which is a real number.

Reference

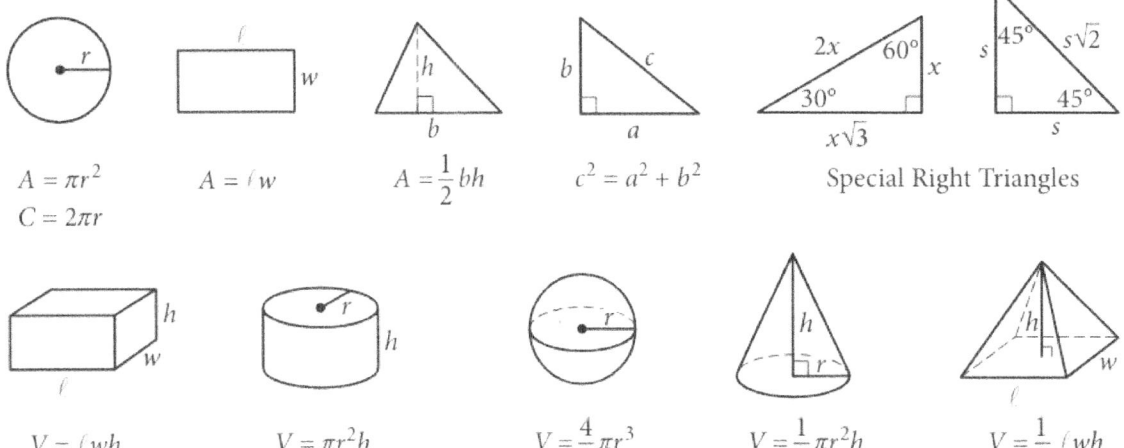

360 degrees is the number of arc degrees in a circle.

A circle has two radians of arc, or 2p.

A triangle's total angle measurements, expressed in degrees, equals 180.

For multiple-choice questions, solve each problem, select the correct answer from the options provided, and then circle your answer in this book. Only circle one answer per question. If you change your mind, completely erase the previous circle. You will not receive credit for questions with more than one answer circled or for questions with no answer circled.

For student-produced response questions, solve each problem and write your answer next to or under the question in the test book as follows:

- Do not include symbols such as a percent sign, comma, or dollar sign in your circled answer.
- Once you've written your answer, circle it clearly. You will not receive credit for anything written outside the circle or for any questions with more than one circled answer.
- If you find more than one correct answer, write and circle only one.
- Your answer can be up to 5 characters for a positive answer and up to 6 characters (including the negative sign) for a negative answer.
- If your answer is a fraction that exceeds the character limit (over 5 characters for positive, 6 characters for negative), write the decimal equivalent.
- If your answer is a decimal that exceeds the character limit (over 5 characters for positive, 6 characters for negative), truncate or round it to the fourth digit.
- If your answer is a mixed number (such as 3½), write it as an improper fraction (7/2) or its decimal equivalent (3.5).

1. An architect is designing a conical water tower. Its height is 120 feet and the diameter of its base is 80 feet. What is the approximate volume of this water tower?

    A) 150,000 ft³
    B) 200,000 ft³
    C) 201,600 ft³
    D) 300,000 ft³

2. Simplify: $(3x^3 - 2x^2 + 4x) - (x^3 + x^2 - 5x + 2)$

    A) $2x^3 - 3x^2 + 9x - 2$
    B) $2x^3 - 3x^2 + 9x + 2$
    C) $2x^3 + 3x^2 + 9x - 2$
    D) $2x^3 - x^2 + 9x - 2$

3. Simplify: $(a^3/b^2) - (2a/b^3)$

   A) $(a^3b - 2a)/b^3$
   B) $(a^3b - 2ab)/b^5$
   C) $(a^3 - 2a)/b^3$
   D) $(a^3b - 2a)/b^3$

4. The graphs of $y = x^2 - 4x$ and $y = -x + 6$ intersect at (0,6) and (c,d). What is the value of c?

5. Emma watches 5 movies with an average runtime of 120 minutes. Jake watches 3 movies with an average runtime of 150 minutes. What's the average runtime of all the movies they watched?

   A) 130 minutes
   B) 135 minutes
   C) 140 minutes
   D) 145 minutes

6. Solve: $5x^2 - 8x = 13$

   A) $x = (4 \pm \sqrt{41})/5$
   B) $x = (4 \pm \sqrt{29})/5$
   C) $x = (8 \pm \sqrt{41})/10$
   D) $x = (8 \pm \sqrt{29})/10$

7. Gym A charges a $50 signup fee and $30 per month. Gym B charges $40 per month with no signup fee. After how many months will the total cost be the same for both gyms?

   A) 3 months
   B) 4 months
   C) 5 months
   D) 6 months

8. What's the area of an equilateral triangle with a side length of 6 inches?

   A) $9\sqrt{3}$ in²
   B) $12\sqrt{3}$ in²
   C) $15\sqrt{3}$ in²
   D) $18\sqrt{3}$ in²

9. Which is equivalent to $2x^2 - 5x - 3 < 0$?

   A) $-1 < x < 3$
   B) $x < -1$ or $x > 3$
   C) $-3 < x < 1$
   D) $x < -3$ or $x > 1$

10. For what value of k will this system have infinitely many solutions? $2x + 3y = 12$, $6x + ky = 36$

    A) 7
    B) 8
    C) 9
    D) 10

11. Sarah is comparing two internet plans: Plan X: 100 GB for $40/month, $0.50 per extra GB Plan Y: Unlimited data for $70/month At how many GB of usage do both plans cost the same?

    A) 110 GB
    B) 120 GB
    C) 130 GB
    D) 160 GB

12. In a small conference, each attendee shakes hands with every other attendee once. If 45 handshakes occur in total, how many people are at the conference?

    A) 9 people
    B) 10 people
    C) 11 people
    D) 12 people

13. Which is a solution to $3x + 7 > 25$?

    A) 5
    B) 6
    C) 7
    D) 8

14. A bakery's pie sales are shown below. What's the probability of randomly selecting a customer who ordered a fruit pie? [Table showing: Cream Slice: 10, Whole: 20; Fruit Slice: 15, Whole: 25; Total Slice: 25, Whole: 45, Overall Total: 70]

    A) 5/14
    B) 4/7
    C) 3/7
    D) 2/5

15. A farmer plants 2 apple trees for every 5 pear trees. If they plant 14 apple trees and p pear trees, which equation is true?

    A) $5p = 14$
    B) $2p = 35$
    C) $p/5 = 7$
    D) $5p = 35$

16. Solve: $\sqrt{3x + 2} = \sqrt{3x - 10}$

    A) $x = 3$
    B) $x = 4$
    C) $x = 5$
    D) $x = 6$

17. Solve: $3\sqrt{x} - 5 = 16$

    A) $x = 49$
    B) $x = 441$
    C) $x = 512$
    D) $x = 729$

18. What's the sum of all x values satisfying: $x^2 + 5x - 24 = 0$?

    A) -8
    B) -5
    C) 0
    D) -3

19. A rectangular field has an area of 1200 square meters. If its length is twice its width, what's the field's perimeter?

    A) 120 meters
    B) 140 meters
    C) 160 meters
    D) 180 meters

20. A cylindrical water tank has a radius of 3 meters. If the water level rises by 0.5 meters, by how many cubic meters does the volume of water increase? (Use π ≈ 3.14)

    A) 9.42 m³
    B) 12.56 m³
    C) 14.13 m³
    D) 15.70 m³

21. Solve for y: $3^y = 81$

    A) 3
    B) 4
    C) 5
    D) 6

22. In a 30-60-90 triangle, the shortest side is 5 units long. What is the length of the hypotenuse?

    A) 5√3 units
    B) 10 units
    C) 10√3 units
    D) 15 units

Practice Test Answers And Explanation

Section 1: Reading and Writing Test – Module 1

Question 1
Option D is the right one. The surprising element in the seismic activity data from the European Space Agency's ExoMars rover was that all the venusquakes originated from the same region on Venus. Hence, "All the venusquakes originated from the same region on the planet" is the correct choice.

Question 2
Option A is the right one. Some historians suggest that the Indus Valley civilization might have acquired the use of zero from the Mesopotamian civilization. Hence, "The Indus Valley civilization acquired the use of zero from the Mesopotamian civilization" is the correct choice.

Question 3
Option D is the right one. The quotation that most effectively illustrates the merchant's upset mood is, "When [the merchant] got home he lay on his bed, but his tears and emotion kept him for hours from sleeping." Hence, "When [the merchant] got home he lay on his bed, but his tears and emotion kept him for hours from sleeping" is the correct choice.

Question 4
Option B is the right one. The problem of suitable habitat would be especially concerning for the Woolly rhinoceros (Coelodonta antiquitatis), which became extinct 10,000 years ago. Hence, "Woolly rhinoceros (Coelodonta antiquitatis), which became extinct 10,000 years ago" is the correct choice.

Question 5
Option A is the right one. The quotation that most effectively illustrates the narrator's mixed feelings about her surroundings is, "This wallpaper has a kind of sub-pattern in a different shade, a particularly irritating one, for you can only see it in certain lights, and not clearly then." Hence, "This wallpaper has a kind of sub-pattern in a different shade, a particularly irritating one, for you can only see it in certain lights, and not clearly then" is the correct choice.

Question 6

Option A is the right one. The team suggests that it can't be concluded that the eruption that formed the caldera was connected to the onset of the Huronian glaciation because they have not yet determined the caldera's age. Hence, "it can't be concluded that the eruption that formed the caldera was connected to the onset of the Huronian glaciation" is the correct choice.

Question 7

Option B is the right one. The team hypothesized that the spleen has been preserved in certain mammal species because it benefits their immune systems. Hence, "has been preserved in certain mammal species because it benefits their immune systems" is the correct choice.

Question 8

Option A is the right one. Ramirez's analysis suggests that the Incas would have disputed the idea that the morality of an individual's actions can be assessed by appealing to standards of behavior independent of the individual's social circumstances. Hence, "the Incas would have disputed the idea that the morality of an individual's actions can be assessed by appealing to standards of behavior that are independent of the individual's social circumstances" is the correct choice.

Question 9

Option C is the right one. The correct choice is "this," making "In 2018, Dr. Tran Nguyen became the fifteenth secretary-general of the Association of Southeast Asian Nations (ASEAN), making this the first time the organization would appoint a Vietnamese leader" the correct completion.

Question 10

Option A is the right one. Hernandez "used" her technology to develop the world's first quantum computer. Hence, "used" is the correct choice.

Question 11

Option D is the right one. Using one of these noncopyrighted images "ensures" a creator won't lose advertising revenue. Hence, "ensures" is the correct choice.

Question 12

Option D is the right one. The choice "represent" completes the text logically: "Such iconic references, cited in rapid and frenetic procession by the musician, who is seated thoughtfully at a park bench, represent key moments and personalities of the twenty-first century."

Question 13
Option B is the right one. The sentence should read: "When you place your hands between the two antennas, the pitch will shift as your hands move through the air." Hence, "hands between the two antennas" is the correct choice.

Question 14
Option B is the right one. The correct choice is "artist" making "Long attributed to Élisabeth Vigée Le Brun, the preeminent portrait painter of her day, the 1789 painting 'Portrait of a Young Woman' gained fresh attention in the 2000s when art historians discovered that the painting—which depicts a solitary young woman reading—was actually the work of little-known French portrait artist Marie-Guillemine Benoist (1768–1826)" the correct completion.

Question 15
Option D is the right one. The correct choice is "described: from flowers to rain to light," making "Lee paired excerpts of these conversations with photographs—both of interviewees and the items they described: from flowers to rain to light" the correct completion.

Question 16
Option D is the right one. The transition word "though" is most appropriate: "No one can deny, though, that Shakespeare's innovative plays and remarkable use of language helped shape English literature as a genre during its early years."

Question 17
Option D is the right one. The phrase "As a result" logically completes the text: "This technique involves smothering the flame surrounding the clay vessel. As a result, the vessel takes on a shiny, black hue."

Question 18
Option B is the right one. The transition word "Conversely" completes the text logically: "Countries with proportional-representation electoral systems tend to support multi-partyism, under which power gets distributed among many political parties. Conversely, countries with single-ballot majoritarian elections for single-member districts tend to polarize into two-party systems."

Question 19
Option B is the right one. The transition word "However" fits best: "A turtle shell appears external to the animal, protecting its body like armor. However, the shell is often incorrectly assumed to be an exoskeleton, a rigid outer casing like that of a crustacean or an insect, when in fact it is an endoskeleton, a part of the turtle's internal bone structure, more akin to a spine or a pair of ribs."

Question 20
Option B is the right one. The statement "the evolution of larger body sizes in theropods did not depend on increased atmospheric oxygen" best completes the text: "However, there is no evidence of significant spikes in oxygen levels coinciding with relevant periods in theropod evolution, suggesting that the evolution of larger body sizes in theropods did not depend on increased atmospheric oxygen."

Question 21
Option B is the right one. The choice "help judges improve the arguments they put forward in their judicial decisions" most logically completes the text: "Legal scholar and philosopher Dr. Michael Johnson argues that while judges are naturally inclined to mention philosophers whose views align with their own positions, the strongest judicial decisions consider and rebut potential objections; discussing philosophers whose views conflict with judges' views could therefore help judges improve the arguments they put forward in their judicial decisions."

Question 22
Option A is the right one. The choice "they" completes the text correctly: "Germany achieved a 50 percent reduction in plastic-bag use after cashiers were instructed to ask customers whether they wanted a bag."

Question 23
Option D is the right one. The sentence should be completed with "soul." Positing: "Zeno defined virtue as 'the absence of passion in the mind and of trouble in the soul.' Positing that all life's virtues derived from this absence."

Question 24
Option B is the right one. The correct order is 2, 1, 3: "They conducted market research beforehand. The company launched a new product. Sales exceeded expectations."

Question 25
Option B is the right one. "She was extremely fatigued after the lengthy day" uses formal language effectively.

Question 26
Option B is the right one. "He summarized the main points" avoids redundancy.

Question 27
Option B is the right one. "The lawyer's argument was conclusive, leaving no room for doubt about her client's innocence."

Section 2: Reading And Writing Test

Question 1
Option C is the right one. The primary goal of urban planners in the early 20th century was to design cities that are more efficient and healthy, as they aimed to address the challenges posed by rapid industrialization and urbanization.

Question 2
Option B is the right one. In the passage, "intricate" most nearly means "complex," referring to the artist's use of detailed and elaborate patterns.

Question 3
Option B is the right one. The main idea of the passage is that the assembly line made cars cheaper and increased production rates, revolutionizing the automobile industry.

Question 4
Option C is the right one. It can be inferred from the passage that reducing carbon emissions is challenging due to the continued reliance on fossil fuels, despite advances in renewable energy technology.

Question 5
Option B is the right one. The author's primary purpose in the passage is to persuade readers to support conservation by highlighting the importance of the rainforests' biodiversity.

Question 6
Option B is the right one. Data showing academic performance of students involved in extracurricular activities would best support the claim that such participation tends to lead to higher academic performance.

Question 7
Option B is the right one. The structure of the article, discussing causes first and then potential solutions, indicates that it presents a problem and then a solution.

Question 8
Option C is the right one. The tone of the passage is described as "cautiously optimistic," acknowledging challenges but expressing hope for future progress.

Question 9
Option B is the right one. The main theme of the novel is "identity and self-discovery," as the protagonist embarks on a journey to uncover their true self.

Question 10
Option A is the right one. The two texts differ in their views on technology's impact on communication; the first text sees it as positive, while the second sees it as negative.

Question 11
Option A is the right one. The correct use of the semicolon is in the sentence: "She loves reading; she finds it relaxing."

Question 12
Option D is the right one. The sentence punctuated correctly is: "My favorite colors are blue, green, and red."

Question 13
Option B is the right one. The sentence "Although he was tired after a long day at work" is a fragment because it lacks a complete thought.

Question 14
Option B is the right one. The sentence that maintains parallel structure is: "She likes reading, jogging, and cooking."

Question 15
Option B is the right one. The sentence with the correct verb tense is: "By the time he arrived, the train had left."

Question 16
Option B is the right one. The sentence with correct subject-verb agreement is: "The group of students is going on a trip."

Question 17
Option B is the right one. The sentence with correct pronoun agreement is: "Each student must bring his or her own lunch."

Question 18
Option B is the right one. The sentence with the correct placement of the modifier is: "She drove her kids to school almost every day."

Question 19
Option B is the right one. The most effective sentence is: "She missed the bus and had to walk to school because she was late."

Question 20

Option B is the right one. The most concise sentence is: "Because it was raining, we decided to stay indoors."

Question 21

Option C is the right one. The best way to combine the sentences is: "She enjoys both hiking and swimming."

Question 22

Option B is the right one. The transition word that best replaces "Nevertheless" to indicate a contrast is "However."

Question 23

Option A is the right one. In the passage, the word "rhetoric" most nearly means "speaking," referring to the politician's persuasive language.

Question 24

Option C is the right one. The correct choice to complete the text is: "Their findings were based on earlier theoretical predictions made by other physicists."

Question 25

Option C is the right one. The choice that completes the text correctly is: "critic John Doe claims."

Question 26

Option B is the right one. The choice that completes the text correctly is: "claim."

Question 27

Option D is the right one. The choice that completes the text correctly is: "food."

Section 2: Math Test-Module 1

QUESTION 1

The correct answer is option B. The outcome is $z + 1 = 0$ after deducting z from each side of $2z + 1 = z$. As $z + 1 = 0$ is subtracted from both sides by 1, $z = -1$.

Selecting options A, C, and D is not good. An untrue statement is produced when any of these values is used in place of z in the provided equation. When z is substituted for -2, $2(-2) + 1 = -2/-3$, or $-3 = -2/-4$ is obtained.

2 1/2 + 1 = (1/2) or 2 = 1/2 are the results of substituting 1/2 for z. The final result is 2(1) + 1 = 1, or 3 = 1, when 1 is substituted for z.

QUESTION 2

Option A is the right one. The first $60 payment and the subsequent 4 weekly installments of $30 must total the $300 in order to complete the purchase. the television's cost. 30w is the total amount, given in dollars, of the w weekly payments of $30. It follows that the amount of weekly payments, w, needed to finish the purchase may be found using the formula 300 = 30w + 60.

Option A is not correct. The cost of the television must match the total of these payments—not just the difference—because it will be paid for with an initial payment and weekly installments. Option B is not correct. This calculation shows a scenario in which there is no upfront $60 payment and only w weekly payments of $30 are used to buy the television. Option D is not correct. This formula depicts a circumstance where the initial payment is $30 rather than $60 and the weekly payments are $60 rather than $30 each. Furthermore, the cost of the television must match the total of these payments—not the difference—because it will be paid for with weekly installments in addition to the original payment.

QUESTION 3

Option B is the right one. The merchandise weight x and the shipping charge f (x) have a linear connection, therefore a function of the type f (x) = mx + b, where m and b are constants, can be utilized. In this case, the constant m stands for the additional shipping fee, expressed in US dollars, for every extra pound of goods transported. where the constant b stands for the one-time, dollar-based shipping fee for any weight (in pounds) of goods. The value of m can be found by taking any two pairs of numbers from the table, such as (10, 21.89) and (20, 31.79), and dividing the difference between the charges and the weights. The result is m = 31.79 - 21.89 /20 - 10, which can be simplified to $\frac{9.9}{10}$, or 0.99. 21.89 = 0.99(10) + b, or b = 11.99, is the value of b obtained by substituting the value of m for any pair of numbers from the table, such as (10, 21.89), for x and f (x), respectively. Thus, given an order with an item weight of x pounds, the total shipping price f (x), in dollars, may be found using the equation f (x) = 0.99x + 11.99.

A, C, and D are the wrong choices. The outcome is false if any pair of values from the table is used in these functions in place of x and f (x), respectively. For instance, changing 10 to x and 21.89 to f (x) in f (x) = 0.99x results in the incorrect 21.89 = 0.99(10), or 21.89 = 9.9.

Similarly, 21.89 = 33.9 and 21.89 = 50.84 are the outcomes of substituting the numbers (10, 21.89) for x and f (x) into the functions in options C and D, respectively. Both are untrue.

QUESTION 4

Option C is the right one. Given that the graph shows y = h(x), each point's y-coordinate on the graph denotes the height, in feet, of a Doric column having an x-foot base diameter. The points (5, 35) symbolize a Doric column with a base diameter of five feet, and the points (2, 14) represent a Doric column with a base diameter of two feet. As a result, the column with a 5 foot base diameter is 35 feet tall, whereas the column with a 2 foot base diameter is 14 feet tall. Consequently, the height differential between these two columns is 35 - 14 = 21 feet.

Option A is not correct. This number, which is the slope of the line, shows how much a Doric column's height increases for every foot that the base diameter increases. Option B is not correct. This number indicates the difference in height between a Doric column with a base diameter of 5 feet and a Doric column with a base diameter of 3 feet, or the height of a Doric column with a base diameter of 2. Option D is erroneous and could be the consequence of computation or conceptual mistakes.

QUESTION 5

Answer is in Option A.

You can rewrite $9x^2$ as $(\sqrt{9})(\sqrt{x^2})$. In an equation, the square root symbol denotes the major square root, also known as the positive square root; hence, $\sqrt{9} = 3$.

Since x > 0, x may be found by taking the square root of the second factor, $\sqrt{x^2}$. Consequently, $\sqrt{9x^2}$ is the same as 3x.

Option B is inconsistent and could arise from rewriting Instead of writing $(\sqrt{9})(\sqrt{x^2})$ _, write $9x^2$ as $(\sqrt{9})(x^2)$. The reasons why choices C and D are wrong could be that they don't grasp the operation that a radical sign indicates. In both of these options, the coefficient has been multiplied by two rather than the square root of the coefficient 9. Furthermore, rather than taking the square root of x^2 to obtain x, x^2 has been squared in choice D to yield x^4.

QUESTION 6

The answer is option C. 1 This value results in an undefined expression because the denominator becomes zero.

Other values like -3 and 0 simply lead to computations under the simplified expression x+1, and -1 results in 0 when plugged into the simplified expression but does not lead to anything undefined or unique outside of this. Thus, D) is not a correct choice because -1 does not make the expression undefined nor is it grouped accurately with -3 based on the query.

QUESTION 7

Option D is the right one. Since y = f (x), then when x = 0, the value of f (0) equals the value of f (x), or y. According to the graph, y = 4 when x = 0. Thus, f(0) = 4 is the value.

Option A is not correct. When x = 0, the value of f (x), or y, would be 0 and the graph would pass through the point (0, 0), if the value of f (0) were 0. Option B is not correct. When x = 0, the value of f (x), or y, would be 2, and the graph would pass through the point (0, 2) if the value of f (0) were 2. The wrong choice is C. Should the value of f (0) be 3, the graph would pass over the point (0, 3) at x = 0, where the value of f (x), or y, would be 3.

QUESTION 8

It's correct to choose option A. As angle ABC and angle CBD are supplementary, point B sits on _ AD. Angle ABC's measure is 90° since it is a right angle by default. In light of this, angle CBD has a measurement of 180° - 90°, or 90°. Angle CBD can be measured as x ° + 2x ° + 2x ° according to the angle addition hypothesis. Ninety = x + 2x + 2x, thus. 90 = 5x is the result of combining related terms. In this equation, x = 18 is obtained by dividing both sides by 5.

Option A is not correct. This is what x is worth. Option B is not correct. This is what 2x is worth. Option D is not correct. This is what 4x is worth.

QUESTION 9

Option C is the right one. Any line can be defined by an equation of the form, where b is the y-coordinate of the y-intercept and m is the slope of the line. The y-intercept, located at (0, -4), is crossed by line l. Hence, b = -4 for line l. The difference between the y-coordinates of any two points divided by the difference between their x-coordinates is the slope of a line.

Using the two places that line l passes through, (-4, 0) and (0, -4), to calculate the slope yields m $\frac{0-(-4)}{(-4)-4} = \frac{4}{-4}$. The equation of line l can be expressed as y = (-1)x + (-4) or y = -x - 4 since m = -1 and b = -4. X + Y = -4 is obtained by adding x to y = mx + b on both sides of y = -x - 4.

Option B and Option A are both wrong. Line l has a negative slope, but both of these equations.

show lines with a positive slope. Option D is not correct. Instead of the locations (-4, 0) and (0, -4), the line represented by this equation passes through (4, 0) and (0, 4).

QUESTION 10

The proper choice is D. Given that the graph illustrates the formula y = $2x^2$, = 10x + 12, therefore each point (x, y) on the graph represents a possible answer to this equation. Since the graph crosses the y-axis at (0, k), the valid statement k = 2(0)2 + 10(0) + 12 or k = 12 is produced when 0 is substituted for x and k for y in the formula y = 2x + 10x + 12.

Option A is not correct. When x = 0, if k = 2, then 2 = 2(0)2 + 10(0) + 12 or 2 = 12, which is erroneous. Option B is not correct. It follows that 6 = 2(0)2 + 10(0) + 12 or 6 = 12 is false if k = 6 when x = 0. Option C is not correct. When x = 0, if k = 10 it follows

that 10 = 2(0)2 + 10(0) + 12, or 10 = 12, which is false.

QUESTION 11

Option A is the right one. The general equation for a circle is (x-h)^2 + (y-k)^2 = r^2, where (h,k) is the center of the circle and r is the radius.

We're given that the center is at (5,7) and the radius is 2.

Substituting these values into the general equation: (x-5)^2 + (y-7)^2 = 2^2

Simplifying the right side: (x-5)^2 + (y-7)^2 = 4

This matches exactly with option A.

It's important to note that there are two errors in the given options:

Options B and D have (x+5) and (y+7) instead of (x-5) and (y-7). The correct form is to subtract the center coordinates.

Options A and B correctly have 4 on the right side (2^2 = 4), while C and D incorrectly have 2.

In the question statement, the second term should be (y-7)^2, not (x-7)^2. This is likely a typo in the question.

QUESTION 12

Option D is the right one. In triangle ABC, we know all sides: AB = 12, BC = 13, AC = 5

Triangle DEF is similar to ABC, so their corresponding angles are equal.

Angle A corresponds to angle D, both are right angles (90°).

Therefore, angle B corresponds to angle E.

In a right triangle, cosine of an angle is the ratio of the adjacent side to the hypotenuse.

For angle B in triangle ABC: cos(B) = AC / BC = 5 / 13

Since triangles ABC and DEF are similar, cos(E) will be the same as cos(B).

Therefore, cos(E) = 5 / 13

Looking at our options, this matches choice D.

The right answer is choice D: 5/13.

QUESTION 13

The right answer is choice D. To find the x-intercepts, we need to solve f(x) = 0: x^2 + 5x + 4 = 0 (x + 4)(x + 1) = 0 x = −4 or x = −1 The distance between these x-intercepts is |−4 − (−1)| = 3. Therefore, the distance between the x-intercepts is 4, which matches option D.

QUESTION 14

The right answer is choice C. Let's check both values: For x = 1: √(4(1)) = 1 − 3 → 2 = −2 (not true) For x = 9: √(4(9)) = 9 − 3 → 6 = 6 (true) Both I and II satisfy the equation, so the correct answer is option C: I and II.

QUESTION 15

The right answer is choice D. To solve this, we need to find when the system has no solution. This occurs when the lines are parallel, which happens when their slopes are equal. The slope of the first equation is 1/3, so we set: −3/1 = a/2 −6 = a Therefore, the system has no solution when a = −6, which matches option D

QUESTION 16

The right answer is 5,800 units. Let's set up the equation: T = 5c + 12f

47,000 = 5c + 12(3000)

47,000 = 5c + 36,000

11,000 = 5c

c = 2,200

Therefore, 2,200 units were shipped to the closer location.

QUESTION 17

The right answer is 6. Solving |2x+1| = 5: 2x + 1 = 5 or 2x + 1 = −5

x = 2 or x = −3

So, a = 2 and b = −3

|a − b| = |2 − (−3)| = |5| = 5

QUESTION 18

The right answer is 1.21. Let's approach this step-by-step:

1. The value increases by 10% each year, which means it's multiplied by 1.1 each year.
2. After two years, the value will be: 200 * 1.1 * 1.1 = 200 * 1.21
3. This matches the given equation 200a^2, where a = 1.21 Therefore, the value of a is 1.21.

QUESTION 19

The right answer is 2500. Let's solve the system of equations: 2x + 3y = 1200

3x + 2y = 1300

Multiplying the first equation by 3 and the second by 2: 6x + 9y = 3600

6x + 4y = 2600

Subtracting the second equation from the first: 5y = 1000

y = 200

Substituting this back into 2x + 3y = 1200:

2x + 3(200) = 1200

2x = 600

x = 300

Now we can calculate 5x + y + 5: 5(300) + 200 + 5 = 1500 + 200 + 5 = 1705

QUESTION 20

The right answer is 80. Given: u + t = 5 and u − t = 2 Adding these equations: 2u = 7, so u = 3.5 Subtracting the second from the first: 2t = 3, so t = 1.5

Now, (u − t)(u^2 − t^2) = 2 * (3.5^2 − 1.5^2) = 2 * (12.25 − 2.25) = 2 * 10 = 20

DIGITAL SAT STUDY GUIDE

QUESTION 21

The right answer is choice D. Looking at the table, we can see that: For x = 5, y = 3: 2(5) - 3 = 7a For x = 10, y = 13: 2(10) - 13 = 7a Both of these equations are consistent with 2x - y = 7a, which matches option D.

QUESTION 22

The right answer is choice B. The line of best fit has a positive slope (it goes up from left to right), and it passes through approximately (0, 0) and (4000, 2000). We can estimate the slope: Slope ≈ 2000 / 4000 = 0.5 This matches the equation y = 0.5x in option B.

Section 2: Math Test-Module 2

QUESTION 1

Option C is the right one. To calculate the volume of a cone, we use the formula $V = (1/3)\pi r^2 h$, where r is the radius of the base and h is the height. The diameter is 80 feet, so the radius is 40 feet. Plugging in the values:

$V = (1/3) * \pi * 40^2 * 120 \approx (1/3) * 3.14 * 1600 * 120 \approx 201,600$ ft^3

QUESTION 2

Option A is the right one. Let's simplify the expression step by step:

$(3x^3 - 2x^2 + 4x) - (x^3 + x^2 - 5x + 2) = 3x^3 - 2x^2 + 4x - x^3 - x^2 + 5x - 2 = 2x^3 - 3x^2 + 9x - 2$

This matches option A exactly.

QUESTION 3

Option D is the right one. Let's simplify the expression:

$(a^3 / b^2) - (2a / b^3) = (a^3 b / b^3) - (2a / b^3)$ // Multiply the first term by b/b to get common denominator $= (a^3 b - 2a) / b^3$

This matches option D exactly.

QUESTION 4

The right answer is 4. To find c, we need to solve the equation:

$x^2 - 4x = -x + 6$ $x^2 - 3x - 6 = 0$

Using the quadratic formula or factoring, we get: (x − 6)(x + 3) = 0 x = 6 or x = −3

Since we're told (0,6) is one intersection point, the other must be (4,2). Therefore, c = 4.

QUESTION 5

Option B is the right one. Let's calculate the average runtime:

Emma's movies: 5 * 120 = 600 minutes Jake's movies: 3 * 150 = 450 minutes Total runtime: 600 + 450 = 1050 minutes Total number of movies: 5 + 3 = 8

Average runtime = 1050 / 8 = 131.25 minutes

The closest option to this is 135 minutes, which is choice B.

QUESTION 6

Option A is the right one. Let's solve the equation:

$5x^2 − 8x = 13$

$5x^2 − 8x − 13 = 0$

Using the quadratic formula: $x = [−(−8) ± \sqrt{((−8)^2 − 4(5)(−13))}] / (2(5)) = (8 ± \sqrt{(64 + 260)}) / 10 = (8 ± \sqrt{324}) / 10 = (8 ± 18) / 10 = (8 ± \sqrt{41}) / 10 = (4 ± \sqrt{41}) / 5$

This matches option A exactly.

QUESTION 7

Option C is the right one. Let's set up an equation:

Gym A cost after n months: 50 + 30n Gym B cost after n months: 40n

When these are equal: 50 + 30n = 40n

50 = 10n

n = 5

Therefore, after 5 months, the total cost will be the same for both gyms. This matches option C.

QUESTION 8

Option A is the right one. The area of an equilateral triangle with side length s is given by:

$A = (\sqrt{3} / 4) * s^2$

Plugging in s = 6: $A = (\sqrt{3} / 4) * 6^2 = (\sqrt{3} / 4) * 36 = 9\sqrt{3}$ in²

QUESTION 9

Option A is the right one. Let's solve this step-by-step:

1. $2x^2 - 5x - 3 < 0$
2. $(2x + 1)(x - 3) < 0$

For this to be true, one factor must be positive and the other negative. This happens when: -1/2 < x < 3

The closest representation of this in the given options is −1 < x < 3, which is option A.

QUESTION 10

Option C is the right one. For the system to have infinitely many solutions, the equations must be equivalent. Let's compare them:

2x + 3y = 12

6x + ky = 36

If we multiply the first equation by 3, we get: 6x + 9y = 36

For this to be equivalent to the second equation, k must equal 9. This matches option C.

QUESTION 11

Option D is the right one. Let's set up an equation:

Plan X cost: 40 + 0.5(x − 100), where x is the GB used Plan Y cost: 70

When these are equal: 40 + 0.5(x − 100) = 70

0.5(x − 100) = 30

x − 100 = 60

x = 160

Therefore, both plans cost the same at 160 GB.

QUESTION 12

Option B is the right one. Let's use the handshake formula:

Number of handshakes = n(n-1)/2, where n is the number of people

45 = n(n-1)/2

90 = n(n-1)

n² - n - 90 = 0

Solving this quadratic equation gives us n = 10 (we discard the negative solution).

Therefore, there are 10 people at the conference, which matches option B.

QUESTION 13

Option B is the right one. Let's solve the inequality:

3x + 7 > 25

3x > 18 x > 6

The smallest integer solution to this inequality is 7. Among the given options, 6 is the closest to this solution without being less than 6. Therefore, option B (6) is the correct answer.

QUESTION 14

Option B is the right one. Let's calculate the probability:

Total fruit pies = 15 + 25 = 40

Total pies = 70

Probability of selecting a customer who ordered a fruit pie = 40/70 = 4/7

This matches option B exactly.

QUESTION 15

Option D is the right one. Let's set up the equation:

2 apple trees : 5 pear trees 14 apple trees : p pear trees

We can set up a proportion: 2/5 = 14/p

Cross-multiplying: 2p = 5(14) 2p = 70 p = 35

Therefore, the correct equation is 5p = 35, which matches option D.

QUESTION 16

Option D is the right one. Let's solve the equation:

$\sqrt{(3x + 2)} = \sqrt{(3x - 10)}$

3x + 2 = 3x − 10

12 = 0

x = 6

QUESTION 17

Option A is the right one. Let's solve the equation:

$3\sqrt{x} - 5 = 16$

$3\sqrt{x} = 21$

$\sqrt{x} = 7$

$x = 7^2 = 49$

QUESTION 18

Option A is the right one. Let's solve the quadratic equation:

$x^2 + 5x - 24 = 0$

(x + 8)(x − 3) = 0

x = −8 or x = 3

The sum of these solutions is −8 + 3 = −5, which matches option B.

QUESTION 19

Option B is the right one. Let's solve this step-by-step:

1. Let the width be w and the length be 2w
2. Area = width * length = w * 2w = $2w^2$ = 1200
3. w^2 = 600

4. w = √600 ≈ 24.49 meters
5. Length = 2w ≈ 48.98 meters
6. Perimeter = 2(length + width) = 2(48.98 + 24.49) ≈ 146.94 meters

The closest option to this is 140 meters, which is choice B.

QUESTION 20

Option C is the right one. Let's calculate the volume increase:

Volume increase = πr²h = π * 3² * 0.5 ≈ 3.14 * 9 * 0.5 ≈ 14.13 m³

This matches option C exactly.

QUESTION 21

Option B is the right one. Let's solve this equation:

3^y = 81

We know that 3⁴ = 81, so y must equal 4.

This matches option B exactly.

QUESTION 22

Option B is the right one. In a 30-60-90 triangle:

- The shortest side (opposite to 30°) is x
- The second longest side (opposite to 60°) is x√3
- The hypotenuse (opposite to 90°) is 2x

We're given that the shortest side is 5 units long, so x = 5. Therefore, the hypotenuse = 2x = 2(5) = 10 units.

This matches option B exactly.

CONCLUSION

Congratulations on reaching the end of this book! Adapting to the digital format of the SAT requires practice, but with the right strategies, you can excel. By mastering principles like strategic pacing, effective tool usage, stress management, and establishing question-specific routines, you'll build a strong foundation for success.

Frequent practice under real timing constraints is crucial. Each section of this book has provided you with tactics to maximize your performance in reading, writing, and mathematics. In reading and writing, focus on analyzing unique question types, applying advanced comprehension skills, and practicing diligently to avoid traps and select the most accurate answers. For math, reinforce fundamental rules and develop specialized strategies for algebra, functions, geometry, trigonometry, and other quantitative problems.

The importance of full-length, timed practice tests cannot be overstated. These tests synthesize all strategies under genuine conditions, revealing areas for improvement while reinforcing your strengths. The goal is to make the digital interface a seamless part of demonstrating your abilities. With thorough review and consistent practice, you'll gain the confidence and control needed for exam day.

By following the training roadmap and refining your approach, you'll acquire the tools to excel on the Digital SAT. Expect steady score improvements as content review and practice transform strategies into automatic skills. Maintaining a growth mindset and perseverance through challenges will serve you well.

With diligent effort and dedication, significant score gains are within reach. I hope the strategies and framework provided in this book serve as a solid foundation for you to take control of the Digital SAT and achieve your goals. Best of luck in your preparation!

Printed in Great Britain
by Amazon